Fix-It and Forget-It®
INSTANT POT
Light & Healthy Cookbook

7-Ingredient Recipes for Weight Loss and Heart Health

HOPE COMERFORD

Photographs by Bonnie Matthews

Good Books

New York, New York

Copyright © 2022 by Good Books
Photos by Bonnie Matthews

All rights reserved. No part of this book may be reproduced in any manner without the express written consent of the publisher, except in the case of brief excerpts in critical reviews or articles. All inquiries should be addressed to Good Books, 307 West 36th Street, 11th Floor, New York, NY 10018.

Good Books books may be purchased in bulk at special discounts for sales promotion, corporate gifts, fund-raising, or educational purposes. Special editions can also be created to specifications. For details, contact the Special Sales Department, Good Books, 307 West 36th Street, 11th Floor, New York, NY 10018 or info@skyhorsepublishing.com.

Good Books is an imprint of Skyhorse Publishing, Inc.®, a Delaware corporation.

Visit our website at www.goodbooks.com.

10 9 8 7 6 5 4 3 2

Library of Congress Cataloging-in-Publication Data is available on file.

Cover design by Laura Klynstra
Cover photo by Meredith Special Interest Media

Print ISBN: 978-1-68099-747-7
Ebook ISBN: 978-1-68099-795-8

Printed in China

Contents

Welcome to *Fix-It and Forget-It Instant Pot Light & Healthy Cookbook* ℚ 1

What Is an Instant Pot? ℚ 1

Getting Started with Your Instant Pot ℚ 2

Instant Pot Tips and Tricks and Other Things You May Not Know ℚ 4

Instant Pot Accessories ℚ 6

What Qualifies as a Seven-Ingredient Recipe? ℚ 6

Light & Healthy Pantry Staples ℚ 8

Breakfast ℚ 9

Soups, Stews & Chilies ℚ 31

Main Dishes ℚ 81

Side Dishes ℚ 139

Desserts ℚ 169

Snacks ℚ 185

Breads/Muffins ℚ 193

Metric Equivalent Measurements ℚ 200

Recipe and Ingredient Index ℚ 201

About the Author ℚ 210

Welcome to Fix-It and Forget-It Instant Pot Light & Healthy Cookbook

Instant Pots have become a staple in many households in recent years. Known for its quick cook time and convenience, the Instant Pot is making life a lot easier for home cooks and families everywhere. Just like any new appliance, it can take some getting used to. However, with a little patience and practice, you'll be an Instant Pot pro in no time at all!

This book has 127 light and healthy recipes to help you get started with a healthier lifestyle, or to help you to continue to cook light and healthy recipes for yourself and your family. What makes these recipes light and healthy? Well, it depends on your definition of healthy. Some people are choosing a low-carb lifestyle; some are choosing to focus on whole grains, some are focusing on low-fat, low-sodium or low-sugar diets; and some are looking for gluten-free recipes. No matter what you deem "healthy," you are sure to find what you're looking for in this book. Please feel free to use margarine instead of butter, coconut oil instead of olive oil, gluten-free flour instead of regular flour, nondairy milk instead of milk, etc. Make the changes you need to the recipes to suit your healthful choices. I've said it before, and I'll say it a million more times: make recipes work for you and your family. If you don't care for an ingredient, omit if possible, or swap it out for something else you do enjoy.

Each recipe in this book contains seven main ingredients or fewer. In a section labeled "Light and Healthy Pantry Staples" below, you will find a list of staple ingredients you will always want to have plenty of on hand for the recipes in this book. The items on this list are *not* included in the seven-ingredient recipe count. Don't worry, these are mainly spices, rice, oil and a few baking staples. Everything else you need for each recipe will be listed in a handy grocery list on each recipe page.

So, dust off that Instant Pot, pull it out of the box, or grab one at the store and get cooking!

What Is an Instant Pot?

In short, an Instant Pot is a digital pressure cooker that also has multiple other functions. Not only can it be used as a pressure cooker, but depending on which model Instant Pot you have, you can set it to do things like sauté, steam, and slow cook. You can cook rice, grains, porridge, soup/stew, beans/chili, meat, poultry, cake, eggs, and yogurt. Because the Instant Pot has so many functions, it takes away the need for multiple appliances on your counter and lets you use fewer pots and pans.

Getting Started with Your Instant Pot

Get to Know Your Instant Pot . . .

The very first thing most Instant Pot owners do is called the water test. It helps you get to know your Instant Pot a bit and might even take a bit of your apprehension away.

Step 1: Plug in your Instant Pot. This may seem obvious to some, but when we're nervous about using a new appliance, sometimes we forget things like this.

Step 2: Make sure the inner pot is inserted in the cooker. You should *never* attempt to cook anything in your device without the inner pot, or you will ruin your Instant Pot. Food should never come into contact with the actual housing unit.

Step 3: The inner pot has lines for each cup (how convenient, right?!). Fill the inner pot with water until it reaches the 3-cup line.

Step 4: Check the sealing ring to be sure it's secure and in place. You should not be able to move it around. If it's not in place properly, you may experience issues with the pot letting out a lot of steam while cooking, or not coming to pressure.

Step 5: Seal the lid. There is an arrow on the lid between and "open" and "close." There is also an arrow on the top of the base of the Instant Pot between a picture of a locked lock and an unlocked lock. Line those arrows up, then turn the lid toward the picture of the lock (left). You will hear a noise that will indicate the lid is locked. If you do not hear a noise, it's not locked. Try it again.

Step 6: *Always* check to see if the steam valve on top of the lid is turned to "sealing." If it's not on "sealing" and is on "venting," it will not be able to come to pressure.

Step 7: Press the "Steam" button and use the +/- arrow to set it to 2 minutes. Once it's at the desired time, you don't need to press anything else. In a few seconds, the Instant Pot will begin all on its own. For those of us with digital slow cookers, we have a tendency to look for the "start" button, but there isn't one on the Instant Pot.

Step 8: Now you wait for the "magic" to happen! The "cooking" will begin once the device comes to pressure. This can take anywhere from 5 to 30 minutes, in my experience. Then, you will see the countdown happen (from the time you set it at). After that, the Instant Pot will beep, which means your meal is done!

Step 9: Your Instant Pot will now automatically switch to "warm" and begin a count of how many minutes it's been on warm. The next part is where you either wait for the NPR, or natural pressure release (the pressure releases all on its own) or you do what's called a QR, or quick release (you manually release the pressure). Which method you choose depends on what you're cooking, but in this case, you can choose either since it's just water. For NPR, you will wait for the lever to move all the way back over to "venting" and watch the pinion (float valve) next to the lever. It will be flush with the lid when at full pressure and will drop when the pressure is done releasing. If you choose QR, be very careful not to have your hands over the vent, as the steam is very hot and you can burn yourself.

The Three Most Important Buttons You Need to Know About . . .

You will find the majority of recipes will use the following three buttons:

Manual/Pressure Cook: Some older models tend to say "Manual," and the newer models seem to say "Pressure Cook." They mean the same thing. From here, you use the +/- button to change the cook time. After several seconds, the Instant Pot will begin its process. The exact name of this button will vary depending on your model of Instant Pot.
Sauté: Many recipes will have you sauté vegetables or brown meat before beginning the pressure cooking process. For this setting, you will not use the lid of the Instant Pot.
Keep Warm/Cancel: This may just be the most important button on the Instant Pot. When you forget to use the +/- buttons to change the time for a recipe, or you press a wrong button, you can hit "keep warm/cancel" and it will turn your Instant Pot off for you.

What Do All the Buttons Do?

With so many buttons, it's hard to remember what each one does or means. You can use this as a quick guide in a pinch.

+/- Buttons. Adjust the cook time up [+] or down [-]. (On newer models, you can also press and hold [-] or [+] for 3 seconds to turn sound OFF or ON.)
Bean/Chili. This button cooks at high pressure for 30 minutes. It can be adjusted using the +/- buttons to cook more for 40 minutes, or less for 25 minutes.
Cake. This button cooks at high pressure for 30 minutes. It can be adjusted using the +/- buttons to cook more for 40 minutes, or less for 25 minutes.
Egg. This button cooks at high pressure for 5 minutes. It can be adjusted using the +/- buttons to cook more for 6 minutes, or less for 4 minutes.

Less | Normal | More. Adjust between the *Less | Normal | More* settings by pressing the same cooking function button repeatedly until you get to the desired setting. (Older versions use the *Adjust* button.)

Meat/Stew. This button cooks at high pressure for 35 minutes. It can be adjusted using the +/- buttons to cook more for 45 minutes, or less for 20 minutes.

Multigrain. This button cooks at high pressure for 40 minutes. It can be adjusted using the +/- buttons to cook more for 45 minutes of warm water soaking time and 60 minutes pressure cooking time, or less for 20 minutes.

Porridge. This button cooks at high pressure for 20 minutes. It can be adjusted using the +/- buttons to cook more for 30 minutes, or less for 15 minutes.

Poultry. This button cooks at high pressure for 15 minutes. It can be adjusted using the +/- buttons to cook more 30 minutes, or less for 5 minutes.

Rice. This button cooks at low pressure and is the only fully automatic program. It is for cooking white rice and will automatically adjust the cooking time depending on the amount of water and rice in the cooking pot.

Soup/Broth. This button cooks at high pressure for 30 minutes. It can be adjusted using the +/- buttons to cook more for 40 minutes, or less for 20 minutes.

Steam. This button cooks at high pressure for 10 minutes. It can be adjusted using the +/- buttons to cook more for 15 minutes, or less for 3 minutes. Always use a rack or steamer basket with this function, because it heats at full power continuously while it's coming to pressure, and you do not want food in direct contact with the bottom of the pressure cooking pot or it will burn. Once it reaches pressure, the steam button regulates pressure by cycling on and off, similar to the other pressure buttons.

Instant Pot Tips and Tricks and Other Things You May Not Know

- Never attempt to cook directly in the Instant Pot without the inner pot!
- Once you set the time, you can walk away. It will show the time you set it to, then will change to the word "on" while the pressure builds. Once the Instant Pot has come to pressure, you will once again see the time you set it for. It will count down from there.
- Always make sure your sealing ring is securely in place. If it shows signs of wear or tear, it needs to be replaced.
- Have a sealing ring for savory recipes and a separate sealing ring for sweet recipes. Many people report their desserts tasting like a roast (or another savory food) if they try to use the same sealing ring for all recipes.

- The stainless-steel rack (trivet) your Instant Pot comes with can used to keep food from being completely submerged in liquid, like baked potatoes or ground beef. It can also be used to set another pot on, for pot-in-pot cooking.
- If you use warm or hot liquid instead of cold liquid, you may need to adjust the cooking time, or your food may not come out done.
- Always double-check to see that the valve on the lid is set to "sealing" and not "venting" when you first lock the lid. This will save you from your Instant Pot not coming to pressure.
- Use Natural Pressure Release for tougher cuts of meat, recipes with high starch (like rice or grains), and recipes with a high volume of liquid. This means you let the Instant Pot naturally release pressure. The little bobbin will fall once pressure is released completely.
- Use Quick Release for more delicate cuts of meat and vegetables. This means you manually turn the vent (being careful not to put your hand over the vent) to release the pressure. The little bobbin will fall once pressure is released completely.
- Make sure there is a clear pathway for the steam to release. The last thing you want is to ruin the bottom of your cupboards with all that steam.
- You *must* use liquid in your Instant Pot. The *minimum* amount of liquid you should have in your inner pot is ½ cup; however, most recipes work best with at least 1 cup.
- Do *not* overfill your Instant Pot! It should only be ½ full for rice or beans (food that expands greatly when cooked) or ⅔ of the way full for most everything else. Do not fill it to the max filled line.
- In this book, the Cooking Time *does not* take into account the amount of time it will take your Instant Pot to come to pressure or the amount of time it will take the Instant Pot to release pressure. Be aware of this when choosing a recipe to make.
- If your Instant Pot is not coming to pressure, it's usually because the sealing ring is not on properly or the vent is not set to "sealing."
- The more liquid, or the colder the ingredients, the longer it will take for the Instant Pot to come to pressure.
- Always make sure that the Instant Pot is dry before inserting the inner pot, and make sure the inner pot is dry before inserting it into the Instant Pot.
- Use a binder clip to hold the inner pot tight against the outer pot when sautéing and stirring. This will keep the pot from "spinning" in the base.
- Doubling a recipe does not change the cook time, but instead it will take longer to come up to pressure.
- You do not always need to double the liquid when doubling a recipe. Depending on what you're making, more liquid may make your food too watery. Use your best judgment.

- When using the slow-cooker function, use the following chart:

Slow Cooker	Instant Pot
Warm	Less or Low
Low	Normal or Medium
High	More or High

Instant Pot Accessories

Most Instant Pots come with a stainless-steel trivet. This will be used in many recipes. Below, you will find a list of accessories that will be used in this cookbook. Most of these accessories can be purchased in-store or online easily from several retailers.

- Extra sealing rings
- Glass lid
- Seven-inch nonstick Bundt cake pan
- Seven-inch springform cake pan (nonstick or silicone)
- Silicone cupcake type molds
- Silicone egg bite molds
- Six ramekins
- Six- and 7-inch round baking pans
- Trivet and/or steamer basket (stainless steel or silicone)

What Qualifies as a Seven-Ingredient Recipe?

- A recipe that has seven or fewer ingredients.
- Spices do not count.
- Water does not count.
- Items listed under "Light & Healthy Pantry Staples" do not count.
- *Optional* ingredients do not count.
- Serving Suggestion items, such as rice, whole-grain pasta, etc. do not count.

Light & Healthy Pantry Staples

The following are ingredients that are commonly used in this Light & Healthy Cookbook. These are items you will consistently need for the recipes in this cookbook. If you always keep these items on hand, you'll just need a few more ingredients for each recipe. To simplify things for you, each recipe will have a "grocery list" of the things you will need beyond these pantry staples.

Pantry Staples

Baking powder

Baking soda

Brown rice

Brown sugar

Cornstarch

Eggs and/or egg substitute

Fresh garlic

Fresh onions

Honey

Low-fat milk, unsweetened almond milk, or milk of your choice

Low-sodium and/or low-fat chicken stock or broth

Low-sodium and/or low-fat vegetable stock or broth

Maple syrup

Margarine and/or butter

Olive oil, grapeseed oil, coconut oil, or canola oil

Turbinado sugar, or sugar of your choice

Vanilla extract

Dried Spices

Basil

Bay leaves

Chili powder

Cinnamon

Coriander, ground

Cumin

Curry

Garlic powder

Kosher salt or sea salt

Nutmeg

Oregano

Paprika

Pepper, black

Thyme

Please note: The recipes in this book are intended for a 6-qt. Instant Pot.

Breakfast

Cinnamon French Toast

Hope Comerford, Clinton Township, MI

Makes 8 servings
Prep. Time: 10 minutes ⚜ Cooking Time: 20 minutes ⚜ Setting: Manual
Pressure: High ⚜ Release: Natural then Manual

3 eggs

2 cups low-fat milk

2 tablespoons maple syrup

15 drops liquid stevia

2 teaspoons vanilla extract

2 teaspoons cinnamon

Pinch salt

16 ounces whole wheat bread, cubed and left out overnight to go stale

Nonstick cooking spray

1½ cups water

Serving Suggestion:
Serve with fat-free whipped cream and a bit of fresh fruit on top, with an extra sprinkle of cinnamon.

1. In a medium bowl, whisk together the eggs, milk, maple syrup, stevia, vanilla, cinnamon, and salt. Stir in the cubes of whole wheat bread.

2. You will need a 7-inch round baking pan for this. Spray the inside with nonstick cooking spray, then pour the bread mixture into the pan.

3. Place the trivet in the bottom of the inner pot, then pour in the water.

4. Carefully place the 7-inch pan on top of the trivet.

5. Secure the lid to the locked position, then make sure the vent is turned to sealing.

6. Press the Manual button and use the "+/-" button to set the Instant Pot for 20 minutes.

7. When the cooking time is over, let the Instant Pot release naturally for 5 minutes, then manually release the rest or the pressure.

Non-Pantry-Staple Grocery List
- 15 drops liquid stevia
- 16 ounces whole wheat bread

Calories 229
Fat 7g
Fiber 4 g
Carbs 35g
Net carbs 31 g
Sodium 453 mg
Sugar 3 g
Protein 9 g

Giant Healthy Pancake

Hope Comerford, Clinton Township, MI

Makes 4 servings
Prep. Time: 10 minutes ❧ Cooking Time: 17 minutes ❧ Setting: Manual
Pressure: Low ❧ Release: Manual

¾ cup whole wheat flour

¼ cup all-purpose flour

¾ teaspoon baking powder

¾ teaspoon baking soda

1 large egg

1¼ cups unsweetened almond milk

1½ tablespoons unsweetened applesauce

Nonstick cooking spray

1 cup water

Non-Pantry-Staple Grocery List
- ¾ cup whole wheat flour
- ¼ cup all-purpose flour
- 1½ tablespoons unsweetened applesauce

Calories 173

Fat 2.8 g

Fiber 3.5 g

Carbs 33 g

Net carbs 29.5 g

Sodium 475 mg

Sugar 9 g

Protein 6 g

1. In a bowl, mix the whole wheat flour, all-purpose flour, baking powder, and baking soda.

2. In a smaller bowl, mix the egg, milk, and unsweetened applesauce until well combined. Pour into the dry ingredients and stir until well combined.

3. Spray a 7-inch round springform pan with nonstick cooking spray and then pour the pancake batter into it.

4. Pour the water into the inner pot of the Instant Pot. Place the springform pan on the trivet and carefully lower the trivet into the inner pot.

5. Secure the lid and make sure the vent is set to sealing.

6. Manually set your Instant Pot to low pressure and set the cook time for 17 minutes.

7. When the cook time is over, manually release the pressure.

8. Remove the lid and carefully lift the trivet out with oven mitts.

9. Remove the cake from the pan and allow to cool for a few minutes before serving and to allow the moisture on the surface of the cake to dry.

Serving Suggestion:

Serve with maple syrup, a drizzle of honey, or topped with your favorite fruit.

Pumpkin Spice Pancake Bites

Hope Comerford, Clinton Township, MI

Makes 14 pancake bites
Prep. Time: 10 minutes   ❧   Cooking Time: 14 minutes   ❧   Setting: Manual
Pressure: High   ❧   Release: Natural then Manual

1 cup gluten-free cup-for-cup flour

1 teaspoon baking powder

$\frac{1}{2}$ teaspoon baking soda

$\frac{1}{2}$ teaspoon cinnamon

$\frac{1}{4}$ teaspoon ground ginger

$\frac{1}{4}$ teaspoon nutmeg

Pinch salt

$\frac{3}{4}$ cup pumpkin puree

1 cup unsweetened almond milk

1 teaspoon vanilla extract

1 large egg, beaten

Nonstick cooking spray

1$\frac{1}{2}$ cups water

Non-Pantry-Staple Grocery List
- 1 cup gluten-free cup-for-cup flour
- $\frac{1}{4}$ teaspoon ground ginger
- $\frac{3}{4}$ cup pumpkin puree

Calories 144

Fat 3 g

Fiber 4.5 g

Carbs 27 g

Net carbs 22.5 g

Sodium 359 mg

Sugar 2.7 g

Protein 4.5 g

1. In a mixing bowl, combine the gluten-free flour, baking powder, baking soda, cinnamon, ginger, nutmeg, and salt.

2. Stir in the pumpkin, almond milk, vanilla, and egg until all ingredients are well mixed.

3. Spray 2 silicone egg bite molds with nonstick cooking spray. Place 2 tablespoons of batter into each cup of the molds. Cover each filled egg bite mold tightly with foil.

4. Pour the water into the inner pot of the Instant Pot and set the trivet on top.

5. Stack the filled silicone egg molds onto one another on top of the trivet in the inner pot.

6. Secure the lid and set the vent to sealing.

7. With the Manual setting, set the cook time to 14 minutes on high pressure.

8. When the cooking time is over, let the pressure release naturally for 5 minutes, then manually release the rest of the pressure.

9. Carefully remove the trivet with oven mitts, uncover the egg bite molds, and pop out your pancake bites onto a plate or serving platter.

Serving Suggestion:
Serve alongside some apple slices and with a bit of maple syrup for dipping the Pumpkin Spice Pancake Bites in.

Insta-Oatmeal

Hope Comerford, Clinton Township, MI

Makes 2 servings
Prep. Time: 2 minutes ❧ Cooking Time: 3 minutes ❧ Setting: Manual
Pressure: High ❧ Release: Manual

1 cup gluten-free rolled oats
1 teaspoon cinnamon
1½ tablespoons maple syrup
Pinch salt
2 cups unsweetened almond milk

1. Place all ingredients in the inner pot of the Instant Pot and give a quick stir.

2. Secure the lid and set the vent to sealing.

3. Press the Manual button and set the cooking time to 3 minutes.

4. When the cooking time is up, manually release the pressure.

5. Remove the lid and stir. If the oatmeal is still too runny for you, let it sit a few minutes uncovered and it will thicken up.

Serving Suggestion:

Top with ¼ cup of your favorite fruits, like banana slices, raspberries, chopped strawberries, or blueberries.

Non-Pantry-Staple Grocery List
• 1 cup gluten-free rolled oats

Calories 270
Fat 6.5 g
Fiber 5.5 g
Carbs 44 g
Net carbs 38.5 g
Sodium 307 mg
Sugar 10 g
Protein 8.5

Scrumptious Breakfast Barley

Hope Comerford, Clinton Township, MI

Makes 4 servings
Prep. Time: 5 minutes ♣ Cooking Time: 18 minutes ♣ Setting: Manual
Pressure: High ♣ Release: Manual

I cup hulled or pearl barley
I tablespoon olive oil
3 cups water
⅓ cup chopped pecans
½ cup dried cranberries
½ teaspoon salt
Maple syrup, *optional*
Unsweetened almond milk, *optional*

TIP
You may exchange the oil for grapeseed, canola, or coconut oil if you wish.

1. Set the Instant Pot to sauté and heat up the oil. Toast barley in the bottom of the inner pot for about 5 minutes, or until it starts to look toasted. Stir continually.

2. Pour in the water and give a little stir.

3. Secure the lid and set the vent to sealing.

4. Manually set the time to cook for 18 minutes on high pressure.

5. When the barley finishes cooking, manually release the pressure and remove the lid.

6. Stir in the pecans, cranberries, and salt, then let stand for 5 to 10 minutes.

7. When serving, top with a little maple syrup and unsweetened almond milk if you wish.

Non-Pantry-Staple Grocery List
• I cup hulled or pearl barley
• ⅓ cup chopped pecans
• ½ cup dried cranberries

Calories 303
Fat 10 g
Fiber 1.5 g
Carbs 14 g
Net carbs 12.5 g
Sodium 274 mg
Sugar 11 g
Protein 4.5

Grain and Fruit Breakfast

Cynthia Haller, New Holland, PA

Makes 4–5 servings

Prep. Time: 5 minutes ❧ Cooking Time: 3 hours ❧ Setting: Slow Cook—Less or Low

$\frac{1}{3}$ cup uncooked quinoa

$\frac{1}{3}$ cup uncooked millet

$\frac{1}{3}$ cup uncooked brown rice

4 cups water

$\frac{1}{4}$ teaspoon salt

$\frac{1}{2}$ cup raisins or dried cranberries

$\frac{1}{4}$ cup chopped nuts, *optional*

1 teaspoon vanilla extract, *optional*

$\frac{1}{2}$ teaspoon ground cinnamon, *optional*

1 tablespoon maple syrup, *optional*

1. Wash the quinoa, millet, and brown rice and rinse well.

2. Place the grains, water, and salt in the inner pot of the Instant Pot. Secure the lid on top.

3. Cook on the Low or Less Slow Cooker setting, or until most of the water has been absorbed, about 3 hours.

4. Add raisins and any optional ingredients and cook for 30 minutes more. If the mixture is too thick, add a little more water.

5. Serve hot or cold.

Serving Suggestion:

Add a little nondairy milk to each bowl of cereal before serving.

Non-Pantry-Staple Grocery List
- $\frac{1}{3}$ cup uncooked quinoa
- $\frac{1}{3}$ cup uncooked millet
- $\frac{1}{3}$ cup uncooked brown rice
- $\frac{1}{2}$ cup raisins or dried cranberries
- $\frac{1}{4}$ cup chopped nuts, *optional*

Calories 230

Fat 5.5 g

Fiber 3.5 g

Carbs 41 g

Net carbs 37.5 g

Sodium 105 mg

Sugar 11.5 g

Protein 5 g

The Perfect Instant Pot Hard-Boiled Eggs

Colleen Heatwole, Burton, MI

Makes 6–8 servings
Prep. Time: 10 minutes   ❧   Cooking Time: 5 minutes   ❧   Setting: Manual
Pressure: High   ❧   Release: Manual

1 cup water

6–8 eggs

1. Pour the water into the inner pot. Place the eggs in a steamer basket, trivet, or egg steamer rack.

2. Close the lid and secure to the locking position. Be sure the vent is turned to sealing. Set for 5 minutes on Manual at high pressure. (It takes about 5 minutes for pressure to build and then 5 minutes to cook.)

3. Let pressure naturally release for 5 minutes, then manually release the remaining pressure.

4. Place the hot eggs into cool water to halt cooking process. You can peel the cooled eggs immediately or refrigerate them unpeeled.

Calories 72
Fat 5 g
Fiber 0 g
Carbs 0 g
Net carbs 0 g
Sodium 71 mg
Sugar 0 g
Protein 6 g

Poached Eggs

Hope Comerford, Clinton Township, MI

Makes 2–4 servings
Prep. Time: 5 minutes ☙ Cooking Time: 2–5 minutes ☙ Setting: Steam
Pressure: High ☙ Release: Manual

1 cup water
Nonstick cooking spray
4 large eggs

1. Place the trivet in the bottom of the inner pot of the Instant Pot and pour in the water.

2. You will need small silicone egg poacher cups that will fit in your Instant Pot to hold the eggs, or a silicone egg bite mold. Spray each silicone cup with nonstick cooking spray.

3. Crack each egg and pour it into the prepared cup.

4. Very carefully place the silicone cups into the Inner Pot so they do not spill.

5. Secure the lid by locking it into place and turn the vent to the sealing position.

6. Push the Steam button and adjust the time— 2 minutes for a very runny egg all the way to 5 minutes for a slightly runny egg.

7. When the timer beeps, release the pressure manually and remove the lid, being very careful not to let the condensation in the lid drip into your eggs.

8. Very carefully remove the silicone cups from the inner pot.

9. Carefully remove the poached eggs from each silicone cup and serve immediately.

Serving Suggestion:
Serve with a toasted piece of whole wheat bread with avocado slices.

Calories 72
Fat 5 g
Fiber 0 g
Carbs 0 g
Net carbs 0 g
Sodium 71 mg
Sugar 0 g
Protein 6 g

Baked Eggs

Esther J. Mast, Lancaster, PA

Makes 8 servings
Prep. Time: 15 minutes   ❧   Cooking Time: 20 minutes   ❧   Setting: Manual
Pressure: High   ❧   Release: Natural   ❧   Standing Time: 10 minutes

1 cup water

2 tablespoons no trans-fat soft margarine, melted

1 cup reduced-fat buttermilk baking mix

1 ½ cups fat-free cottage cheese

2 teaspoons chopped onion

1 teaspoon dried parsley

Salt

½ cup shredded reduced-fat cheddar cheese

1 egg, slightly beaten

1 ¼ cups egg substitute

1 cup fat-free milk

Serving Suggestion:
Serve with low-carb, low-sugar muffins and a fresh fruit cup.

Non-Pantry-Staple Grocery List
- 1 cup reduced-fat buttermilk baking mix
- 1 ½ cups fat-free cottage cheese
- 1 teaspoon dried parsley
- ½ cup shredded reduced-fat cheddar cheese

1. Place the trivet into the bottom of the inner pot and pour in the water.

2. Grease a round 7-inch springform pan that will fit into the inner pot of the Instant Pot.

3. Pour the melted margarine into the springform pan.

4. In a large mixing bowl, mix the buttermilk baking mix, cottage cheese, onion, parsley, salt, cheese, egg, egg substitute, and milk.

5. Pour the mixture over the melted margarine. Stir slightly to distribute the margarine.

6. Place the springform pan onto the trivet, close the lid, and secure to the locking position. Be sure the vent is turned to sealing. Set for 20 minutes on Manual at high pressure.

7. Let the pressure release naturally.

8. Carefully remove the springform pan with the handles of the steaming rack and allow to stand 10 minutes before cutting and serving.

Calories 195
Fat 8 g
Fiber 0.5 g
Carbs 15 g
Net carbs 14.5 g
Sodium 536 mg
Sugar 4 g
Protein 15 g

Delicious Shirred Eggs

Hope Comerford, Clinton Township, MI

Makes 6 servings
Prep. Time: 5 minutes 🔹 Cooking Time: 2–3 minutes 🔹 Setting: Manual
Pressure: Low 🔹 Release: Manual

Nonstick cooking spray

1 garlic clove, minced

2 tablespoons fresh minced onion

6 tablespoons skim milk, *divided*

6 jumbo eggs

6 tablespoons grated fresh Parmesan cheese, *divided*

Fresh cracked pepper

1 cup water

Non-Pantry-Staple Grocery List
• 6 tablespoons freshly grated Parmesan cheese

Calories 113
Fat 8 g
Fiber 0 g
Carbs 2 g
Net carbs 2 g
Sodium 167 mg
Sugar 1 g
Protein 8 g

1. Spray 6 ramekins with nonstick cooking spray.

2. Evenly divide the minced garlic and onion among the 6 ramekins.

3. Pour 1 tablespoon of milk into each ramekin.

4. Break an egg into each ramekin.

5. Top each egg with 1 tablespoon freshly grated cheese.

6. Season with fresh cracked pepper.

7. Pour the water into the inner pot of the Instant Pot. Place the trivet on top.

8. Arrange 3 ramekins on top of the trivet, then carefully stack the remaining 3 ramekins on top, staggering their positions so each ramekin on top is sitting between 2 on the bottom layer.

9. Secure the lid and set the vent to sealing.

10. Set the Instant Pot to low pressure and manually set the cook time to 2 minutes for runny yolks or 3 minutes for hard yolks.

11. When cook time is complete, manually release the pressure, and remove the lid. Serve immediately.

To-Go Crustless Veggie Quiche Cups

Hope Comerford, Clinton Township, MI

Makes 14 mini quiches

Prep. Time: 15 minutes ❧ Cooking Time: 11 minutes ❧ Setting: Manual ❧ Pressure: High
Release: Natural then Manual ❧ Cooling Time: 5 minutes

2 teaspoons olive oil

$\frac{1}{2}$ green bell pepper, diced

$\frac{1}{4}$ cup finely chopped broccoli florets

$\frac{1}{2}$ small onion, diced

5 ounces fresh spinach

Nonstick cooking spray

8 eggs

$\frac{1}{4}$ cup skim milk

3 drops hot sauce, *optional*

$\frac{1}{3}$ cup shredded reduced-fat cheddar cheese

I cup water

TIP
You may replace the olive oil with canola, grapeseed or coconut oil if you wish.

1. In a small pan on the stove, heat 2 teaspoons olive oil over medium-high heat. Sauté the bell pepper, broccoli, and onion for about 8 minutes. Add the spinach and continue to cook until wilted.

2. Spray 2 egg molds with nonstick cooking spray. Divide the cooked vegetables evenly between the egg bite mold cups.

3. In a bowl, whisk the eggs, skim milk, and hot sauce (if using). Divide this evenly between the egg bite mold cups, or until each cup is $\frac{2}{3}$ of the way full. Cover them tightly with foil.

4. Evenly divide the shredded cheese between the cups.

5. Pour the water into the inner pot of the Instant Pot. Place the trivet on top, then place the 2 filled egg bite molds on top of the trivet, the top one stacked staggered on top of the one below.

6. Secure the lid and set the vent to sealing.

Non-Pantry-Staple Grocery List
- $\frac{1}{2}$ green bell pepper
- $\frac{1}{4}$ cup finely chopped broccoli florets
- 5 ounces fresh spinach
- 3 drops hot sauce, *optional*
- $\frac{1}{3}$ cup shredded reduced-fat cheddar cheese

Calories 245
Fat 17 g
Fiber 1 g
Carbs 5 g
Net carbs 4 g
Sodium 305 mg
Sugar 2 g
Protein 17 g

7. Manually set the cook time for 11 minutes on high pressure.

8. When the cook time is up, let the pressure release naturally for 5 minutes, then manually release the remaining pressure.

9. When the pin drops, remove the lid and carefully lift the trivet and molds out with oven mitts.

10. Place the molds on a wire rack and uncover. Let cool for about 5 minutes, then pop them out onto a plate or serving platter.

Serving Suggestion:
Serve alongside your favorite healthy bread and a bowl of fruit.

Easy Quiche

Becky Bontrager Horst, Goshen, IN

Makes 6 servings, 1 slice per serving
Prep. Time: 15 minutes ⚇ Cooking Time: 25 minutes ⚇ Setting: Manual
Pressure: High ⚇ Release: Natural

1 cup water

Nonstick cooking spray

¼ cup chopped onion

¼ cup chopped mushrooms, *optional*

3 ounces shredded reduced-fat cheddar cheese

2 tablespoons bacon bits, chopped ham, or browned sausage

4 eggs

¼ teaspoon salt

1 ½ cups fat-free milk

½ cup whole wheat flour

1 tablespoon trans-fat-free soft margarine

1. Pour the water into the inner pot of the Instant Pot and place the steaming rack inside.

2. Spray a 6-inch round cake pan with nonstick cooking spray.

3. Sprinkle the onion, mushrooms, shredded cheddar, and meat in the cake pan.

4. In a medium bowl, combine the remaining ingredients. Pour them over the meat and vegetables.

5. Place the cake pan onto the steaming rack, close the lid, and secure to the locking position. Be sure the vent is turned to sealing. Set for 25 minutes on Manual at high pressure.

6. Let the pressure release naturally.

7. Carefully remove the cake pan with the handles of the steaming rack and allow to stand 10 minutes before cutting and serving.

Non-Pantry-Staple Grocery List
- 3 ounces shredded reduced-fat cheddar cheese
- 2 tablespoons bacon bits, chopped ham, or browned sausage
- ½ cup whole wheat flour
- ¼ cup chopped mushrooms, *optional*

Calories 145

Fat 7 g

Fiber 1.5 g

Carbs 10 g

Net carbs 8.5 g

Sodium 324 mg

Sugar 1.5 g

Protein 11 g

Breakfast Apples

Hope Comerford, Clinton Township, MI

Makes 4 servings
Prep. Time: 10 minutes ⚘ *Cooking Time: 2 minutes* ⚘ *Setting: Manual*
Pressure: High ⚘ *Release: Manual*

Nonstick cooking spray
4 medium apples, peeled and sliced
¼ cup honey
1 tablespoon chia seeds
1 teaspoon cinnamon
2 tablespoons melted coconut oil
1 cup water
2 cups gluten-free grain-free granola of your choice

1. Spray a 7-inch round cake pan or oven-safe baking dish with nonstick cooking spray. Set aside.

2. In a bowl, combine the apple slices, honey, chia, cinnamon, and coconut oil. Pour into the 7-inch pan.

3. Pour the water into the inner pot of the Instant Pot. Place the trivet in the inner pot, then carefully place the 7-inch pan on top.

4. Secure the lid and set the lid to sealing. Manually set the time to 2 minutes on high pressure.

5. Manually release the pressure when the cook time is over.

6. Carefully remove the trivet with oven mitts, sprinkle the apples with the grain-free granola, and serve.

Non-Pantry-Staple Grocery List
- 4 medium apples
- 1 tablespoon chia seeds
- 2 cups gluten-free grain-free granola

Calories 532
Fat 23 g
Fiber 11 g
Carbs 74 g
Net carbs 63 g
Sodium 18 mg
Sugar 45 g
Protein 10 g

Spinach and Mushroom Frittata

J. B. Miller, Indianapolis, IN

Makes 4 servings

Prep. Time: 5 minutes ❧ Cooking Time: 10 minutes ❧ Setting: Manual
Pressure: High ❧ Release: Natural

6 eggs or egg substitute equivalent to 6 eggs

½ teaspoon salt

¼ teaspoon black pepper

1 tablespoon fresh basil, minced

3 garlic cloves, minced

1 small shallot, minced

½ lb. sliced baby bella mushrooms

10-ounce bag fresh spinach

¼ cup shredded Gruyère cheese

Nonstick cooking spray

1 cup water

1. In a bowl, beat the eggs, salt, and pepper.

2. Gently fold in the basil, garlic, shallot, mushrooms, spinach, and cheese.

3. Spray a 7-inch round pan with nonstick cooking spray, then pour in the egg/vegetable/cheese mixture.

4. Pour the water into the bottom of the inner pot of the Instant Pot.

5. Place the 7-inch round pan on top of the trivet and slowly lower it into the Instant Pot using the handles.

6. Secure the lid and set the valve to sealing.

7. Set the Instant Pot to Manual and set the cooking time to 10 minutes.

8. When the cooking time is over, let the pressure release naturally, then remove the lid and remove the trivet and pan carefully with oven mitts.

9. Slice into 4 slices and serve warm.

Non-Pantry-Staple Grocery List
- 1 tablespoon fresh basil
- 1 small shallot
- ½ lb. sliced baby bella mushrooms
- 10-ounce bag fresh spinach
- ¼ cup shredded Gruyère cheese

Calories 215
Fat 12 g
Fiber 4 g
Carbs 11 g
Net carbs 7 g
Sodium 188 mg
Sugar 3 g
Protein 16 g

Instant Pot Yogurt

Cynthia Hockman-Chupp, Canby, OR

Makes 16 servings

Prep. Time: 10 minutes ❧ *Cooking Time: 8 hours+* ❧ *Setting: Yogurt*

1 gallon low-fat milk

¼ cup low-fat plain yogurt with active cultures

Serving Suggestion:
When serving, top with fruit, granola, or nuts. If you'd like, add a dash of vanilla extract, peanut butter, or other flavoring. We also use this yogurt in smoothies!

Non-Pantry-Staple Grocery List

- ¼ cup low-fat plain yogurt with active cultures

Calories 149
Fat 8 g
Fiber 0 g
Carbs 12 g
Net carbs 12 g
Sodium 105 mg
Sugar 12 g
Protein 8 g

1. Pour the milk into the inner pot of the Instant Pot.

2. Lock the lid, move the vent to sealing, and press the Yogurt button. Press Adjust till it reads "boil."

3. When boil cycle is complete (about 1 hour), check the temperature. It should be at 185°F. If it's not, use the sauté function to warm to 185°F.

4. After it reaches 185°F, press cancel on the Instant Pot, remove inner pot, and cool. You can place on cooling rack and let it slowly cool. If in a hurry, submerge the base of the pot in cool water. Cool milk to 110°F.

5. When mixture reaches 110°F, stir in the ¼ cup of yogurt. Place the inner pot back into the Instant Pot, lock the lid in place, and move the vent to sealing.

6. Press Yogurt. Use the Adjust button until the screen says 8:00. This will now incubate for 8 hours.

7. After 8 hours (when the cycle is finished), chill yogurt, or go immediately to straining in step 8.

8. After chilling, or following the 8 hours, strain the yogurt using a nut milk bag. This will give it the consistency of Greek yogurt.

Soups, Stews & Chilies

White Bean Soup

Esther H. Becker, Gordonville, PA

Makes 6 servings
Prep. Time: 5 minutes ☙ Soaking Time: overnight (optional) ☙ Cooking Time: 9 minutes
Setting: Manual ☙ Pressure: High ☙ Release: Natural

8 ounces (about 1 ¼ cups) dried white beans

4 cups water

3 cups low-fat, low-sodium chicken stock

1 teaspoon grapeseed or olive oil

1 onion, diced

2 cups raw sweet potatoes (about 2 medium potatoes), diced

1 cup green bell pepper, diced

¼ teaspoon ground cloves

¼ teaspoon black pepper

½ teaspoon dried thyme

½ cup low-sugar ketchup

¼ cup molasses

Non-Pantry-Staple Grocery List
- 8 ounces dried white beans
- 2 medium sweet potatoes
- 1 green bell pepper
- ¼ teaspoon ground cloves
- ½ cup low-sugar ketchup
- ¼ cup molasses

Calories 274
Fat 2.5 g
Fiber 8 g
Carbs 51 g
Net carbs 43 g
Sodium 303 mg
Sugar 18 g
Protein 13 g

1. In a pot of water, soak the beans overnight. Drain and rinse. Place drained beans in the inner pot of the Instant Pot.

2. Pour in the water, chicken stock, grapeseed oil, onion, sweet potato, bell pepper, ground cloves, black pepper, and thyme.

3. Secure the lid and set the vent to sealing.

4. Manually set the cook time to 9 minutes at high pressure.

5. When the cooking time is over, allow the pressure to release naturally. When the pin drops, remove the lid.

6. Stir in the ketchup and molasses. Add more water if you would like your soup to be thinner.

TIPS

1. Adding the teaspoon of oil to the pot keeps foam from becoming too great in the pot and clogging the vent.

2. If you don't want to soak the beans, or forget to soak the beans, simply set the cook time to 31 minutes on high pressure.

Cannellini Bean Soup

Hope Comerford, Clinton Township, MI

Makes 6–8 servings
Prep. Time: 10 minutes ⚜ Soaking Time: overnight (optional) ⚜ Cooking Time: 30 minutes
Setting: Sauté then Manual ⚜ Pressure: High ⚜ Release: Natural

2 tablespoons extra-virgin olive oil

4 garlic cloves, sliced very thin

1 small onion, chopped

2 heads escarole, well washed and cut medium-fine (about 8 cups)

8-ounce bag dry cannellini beans, soaked overnight

8 cups low-sodium chicken stock

3 basil leaves, chopped fine

Parmesan cheese shavings, *optional*

1. Set the Instant Pot to Sauté and heat the olive oil.

2. Sauté the garlic, onion, and escarole until the onion is translucent.

3. Hit the Cancel button on your Instant Pot and add the beans and chicken stock.

4. Secure the lid and set the vent to sealing.

5. Manually set the time for 25 minutes on high pressure.

6. When the cooking time is over, let the pressure release naturally. Remove the lid when the pin drops and spoon into serving bowls.

7. Top each bowl with a sprinkle of the chopped basil leaves and a few Parmesan shavings (if using).

Non-Pantry-Staple Grocery List
- 2 heads escarole
- 8-ounce bag cannellini beans
- 3 basil leaves
- Parmesan cheese shavings, *optional*

Calories 221
Fat 6.5 g
Fiber 5 g
Carbs 28 g
Net carbs 23 g
Sodium 353 mg
Sugar 5 g
Protein 13 g

TIPS

1. You may replace the olive oil with canola or grapeseed oil if you wish.

2. If you don't have time to soak the beans overnight, simply cook the soup on high pressure for 51 minutes instead.

Black Bean Soup with Fresh Salsa

Hope Comerford, Clinton Township, MI

Makes 6–8 servings
Prep. Time: 5 minutes ❧ Soaking Time: overnight ❧ Cooking Time: 70 minutes
Setting: Manual ❧ Pressure: High ❧ Release: Natural

8 ounces dry black beans, soaked overnight

7 cups low-sodium chicken stock

5 garlic cloves, minced

1 tablespoon chili powder

1½ teaspoons cumin

1½ teaspoons oregano

1 teaspoon salt

1 teaspoon olive oil

3 tablespoons fat-free sour cream, *optional*

Salsa Ingredients:

⅓ cup fresh cilantro, washed and stemmed

½ onion, coarsely chopped

Juice of ½ lime

¼ teaspoon salt

1. Place the beans, chicken stock, garlic, chili powder, cumin, oregano, salt, and olive oil into the inner pot of the Instant Pot.

2. Secure the lid and set the vent to sealing.

3. Manually set the cook time for 70 minutes on high pressure.

4. While the soup is cooking, puree the cilantro, onion, lime juice, and salt in a food processor until smooth. Place in a small bowl and keep refrigerated until serving time.

5. When the cooking time is over, let the pressure release naturally.

6. When the pin drops, remove the lid and scoop out about 1 cup of cooked beans with a slotted spoon and place in a bowl. Using an immersion blender, puree the beans then stir them back into the pot.

7. Spoon soup into serving bowls and serve with a bit of optional sour cream and fresh salsa on top.

Non-Pantry-Staple Grocery List
- 8-ounce bag black beans
- 3 tablespoons fat-free sour cream, *optional*
- ⅓ cup fresh cilantro
- ½ lime

TIP

Do not skip the olive oil. The oil in the pot keeps the foam from the beans cooking at a minimum to help prevent clogging the vent during cooking. You may replace the olive oil with canola or grapeseed oil instead if you wish.

Calories 190
Fat 4 g
Fiber 5 g
Carbs 27 g
Net carbs 22 g
Sodium 631 mg
Sugar 4.5 g
Protein 12 g

Mediterranean Lentil Soup

Marcia S. Myer, Manheim, PA

Makes 6 servings
Prep. Time: 10 minutes ❧ Cooking Time: 18 minutes ❧ Setting: Manual
Pressure: High ❧ Release: Manual

2 tablespoons olive oil

2 large onions, chopped

1 carrot, chopped

1 cup uncooked lentils

½ teaspoon dried thyme

½ teaspoon dried marjoram

3 cups low-sodium chicken stock or vegetable stock

14.5-ounce can diced no-salt-added tomatoes

¼ cup chopped fresh parsley

¼ cup sherry, *optional*

⅔ cup grated low-fat cheese, *optional*

TIP
You may replace the olive oil with canola or grapeseed oil if you wish.

1. Set the Instant Pot to the Sauté function, then heat up the olive oil.

2. Sauté the onions and carrot until the onions are translucent, about 5 minutes.

3. Press the Cancel button, then add the lentils, thyme, marjoram, chicken stock, and canned tomatoes.

4. Secure the lid and set the vent to sealing.

5. Manually set the cook time to 18 minutes at high pressure.

6. When the cooking time is over, manually release the pressure.

7. When the pin drops, stir in the parsley and sherry (if using).

8. When serving, add a sprinkle of grated low-fat cheese if you wish.

Non-Pantry-Staple Grocery List
- 1 carrot
- 1 cup lentils
- ½ teaspoon dried marjoram
- 14.5-ounce can diced tomatoes
- ¼ cup fresh parsley
- ¼ cup sherry, *optional*
- ⅔ cup grated low-fat cheese, *optional*

Calories 282

Fat 6 g

Fiber 2 g

Carbs 18 g

Net carbs 16 g

Sodium 303 mg

Sugar 6 g

Protein 5 g

Lentil and Barley Soup

Sherri Grindle, Goshen, IN

Makes 10 servings

Prep. Time: 8–10 minutes ♣ *Cooking Time: 10 minutes* ♣ *Setting: Manual*
Pressure: High ♣ *Release: Manual*

2 tablespoons olive oil

2 celery ribs, thinly sliced

1 medium onion, chopped

1 garlic clove, minced

1 cup thinly sliced carrots

28-ounce can no-salt-added diced tomatoes

¾ cup uncooked lentils, rinsed

¾ cup uncooked pearl barley

2 tablespoons (or 3 cubes) low-sodium chicken bouillon granules

½ teaspoon dried oregano

½ teaspoon dried rosemary

¼ teaspoon pepper

6 cups water

1 cup (4 ounces) shredded low-fat Swiss cheese, *optional*

1. Set the Instant Pot to the Sauté function and heat up the olive oil.

2. Sauté the celery, onion, garlic, and carrots for about 5 to 8 minutes in the inner pot.

3. Press Cancel, then add the diced tomatoes, lentils, pearl barley, chicken bouillon granules, oregano, rosemary, pepper, and water to the inner pot.

4. Secure the lid and set the vent to sealing.

5. Manually set the cook time to 10 minutes on high pressure.

6. When the cooking time is over, manually release the pressure.

7. If you wish, sprinkle each serving with 1 rounded tablespoon of cheese when serving.

TIP
You may replace the olive oil with canola or grapeseed oil if you wish.

Non-Pantry-Staple Grocery List
- 2 celery ribs
- 2 carrots
- 28-ounce can no-salt-added diced tomatoes
- ¾ cup lentils
- ¾ cup pearl barley
- 1 tablespoon low-sodium chicken bouillon granules
- ½ teaspoon dried rosemary
- 1 cup shredded low-fat Swiss cheese, *optional*

Calories 164

Fat 5 g

Fiber 3 g

Carbs 24 g

Net carbs 21 g

Sodium 353 mg

Sugar 4 g

Protein 6 g

Lentil, Spinach, and Rice Soup

Jean Harris Robinson, Cinnaminson, NJ

Makes 10 servings

Prep. Time: 5–8 minutes ❧ Cooking Time: 12 minutes ❧ Setting: Manual
Pressure: High ❧ Release: Manual

2 tablespoons extra-virgin olive oil

1 large onion, diced

2 carrots, diced

1 celery rib, diced

1 cup uncooked lentils

6 cups low-sodium chicken stock or vegetable stock

2 cups water

14.5-ounce can diced no-salt-added tomatoes

¼ cup uncooked brown rice

1 bag (about 8 cups) fresh spinach, washed, dried, and chopped (with large stems removed)

TIP

You may replace the olive oil with canola or grapeseed oil if you wish.

1. Set the Instant Pot to Sauté and heat up the olive oil.

2. Sauté the onion, carrots, and celery for 5 to 8 minutes.

3. Press the Cancel button, then add the lentils, stock, water, diced tomatoes with their juices, and brown rice.

4. Secure the lid and set the vent to sealing.

5. Manually set the cook time for 12 minutes on high pressure.

6. When the cooking time is over, you may manually release the pressure.

7. When the pin drops, remove the lid and stir in the spinach. Give it a couple minutes to wilt, then serve and enjoy!

Non-Pantry-Staple Grocery List
- 2 carrots
- 1 celery rib
- 1 cup lentils
- 14.5-ounce can diced tomatoes
- 8 cups fresh spinach

Calories 227
Fat 4 g
Fiber 8 g
Carbs 37 g
Net carbs 29 g
Sodium 313 mg
Sugar 3 g
Protein 11 g

Tomato and Barley Soup

Hope Comerford, Clinton Township, MI

Makes 6 servings
Prep. Time: 5–8 minutes ❧ Cooking Time: 20 minutes ❧ Setting: Manual
Pressure: High ❧ Release: Manual

2 tablespoons olive oil

2 garlic cloves, chopped

1 medium onion, chopped

2 celery ribs, including tops, cut up

1–2 cups sliced fresh mushrooms

¾ cup uncooked medium barley, rinsed

2 (14.5-ounce) cans diced tomatoes

2 tablespoons fresh basil

6 cups low-sodium chicken stock or vegetable stock

1. Set the Instant Pot to the Sauté function, then heat up the olive oil.

2. Sauté the garlic, onion, and celery in the oil for 5 to 8 minutes.

3. Press Cancel, then add the remaining ingredients to the inner pot.

4. Secure the lid and set the vent to sealing.

5. Manually set the cook time to 20 minutes on high pressure.

6. When the cooking time is over, manually release the pressure.

TIP
You may replace the olive oil with canola or grapeseed oil if you wish.

Non-Pantry-Staple Grocery List
- 2 celery ribs
- 1–2 cups sliced mushrooms
- ¾ cup medium barley
- 2 (14.5-ounce) cans diced tomatoes
- 2 tablespoons fresh basil

Calories 260
Fat 8 g
Fiber 5 g
Carbs 37 g
Net carbs 32 g
Sodium 582 mg
Sugar 6 g
Protein 10 g

Indian Tomato Rice Soup

Valerie Drobel, Carlisle, PA

Makes 4–6 servings
Prep. Time: 10 minutes ❧ Cooking Time: 10 minutes ❧ Setting: Sauté and Manual
Pressure: High ❧ Release: Natural then Manual

1 tablespoon olive oil

2 cups chopped onion

3 garlic cloves, minced

1 cup brown basmati rice, rinsed

1 teaspoon cumin

1 teaspoon coriander

6 cups low-sodium chicken stock or vegetable stock

1 lb. fresh tomatoes, chopped

2 tablespoons chopped cilantro

TIP
You may replace the olive oil with canola or grapeseed oil if you wish.

1. Set the Instant Pot to Sauté and heat the olive oil.

2. Sauté the onion and garlic in the heated oil for 3 to 5 minutes.

3. Press Cancel and then add the basmati rice, cumin, coriander, and stock.

4. Secure the lid and set the vent to sealing.

5. Manually set the cook time to 14 minutes on high pressure.

6. When the cooking time is over, allow the pressure to release naturally for 10 minutes, and then manually release the rest of the pressure.

7. When the pin drops, remove the lid and set the Instant Pot to Sauté once more. Stir in the tomatoes and let simmer for about 5 minutes.

8. Add cilantro and serve.

Non-Pantry-Staple Grocery List
- 1 cup brown basmati rice
- 1 lb. fresh tomatoes
- 2 tablespoons fresh chopped cilantro

Calories 259
Fat 6 g
Fiber 3 g
Carbs 40 g
Net carbs 37 g
Sodium 352 mg
Sugar 8 g
Protein 10 g

Creamy Wild Rice Mushroom Soup

Hope Comerford, Clinton Township, MI

Makes 4 servings
Prep. Time: 10 minutes & *Cooking Time: 40 minutes* & *Setting: Manual*
Pressure: High & *Release: Manual*

½ large onion, chopped

3 garlic cloves, chopped

3 celery ribs, chopped

3 carrots, chopped

8 ounces fresh baby bella mushrooms, sliced

I cup wild rice

4 cups low-sodium chicken stock or vegetable stock

½ teaspoon dried thyme

¼ teaspoon pepper

I cup fat-free half-and-half

2 tablespoons cornstarch

2 tablespoons cold water

1. Place the onion, garlic, celery, carrots, mushrooms, wild rice, stock, thyme, and pepper into the inner pot of the Instant Pot and secure the lid. Make sure the vent is set to sealing.

2. Manually set the time for 30 minutes on high pressure.

3. When the cooking time is over, manually release the pressure and remove the lid when the pin drops.

4. While the pressure is releasing, heat the half-and-half either in the microwave or on the stove top.

5. Whisk together the cornstarch and cold water. Whisk this into the heated half-and-half.

6. Slowly whisk the half-and-half/cornstarch mixture into the soup in the Instant Pot. Serve and enjoy!

Non-Pantry-Staple Grocery List
- 3 celery ribs
- 3 carrots
- 8 ounces baby bella mushrooms
- I cup wild rice
- I cup fat-free half-and-half

Calories 301
Fat 4 g
Fiber 7 g
Carbs 54 g
Net carbs 47 g
Sodium 408 mg
Sugar 9 g
Protein 14 g

Potato and Spinach Soup

Jane S. Lippincott, Wynnewood, PA

Makes 6 servings
Prep. Time: 8 minutes ❧ Cooking Time: 14 minutes ❧ Setting: Manual
Pressure: High ❧ Release: Manual

2 tablespoons olive oil

2 celery ribs, chopped

1 medium onion, chopped

1 garlic clove, minced

4 medium russet potatoes, unpeeled and chopped into 1-inch-thick pieces

4 cups low-sodium chicken stock or vegetable stock

1 teaspoon mustard seeds

¼ teaspoon pepper

6 cups chopped fresh spinach

1 tablespoon white wine vinegar

Chopped chives for garnish

TIP
You may replace the olive oil with canola or grapeseed oil if you wish.

1. Set the Instant Pot to Sauté and heat the olive oil in the inner pot.

2. Sauté the celery, onion, and garlic in the heated oil for about 5 minutes.

3. Press Cancel and add the potatoes, stock, mustard seeds, and pepper.

4. Secure the lid and set the vent to sealing.

5. Manually set the cook time for 4 minutes, then manually release the pressure when the cooking time is over.

6. When the pin drops, remove the lid. Use a potato masher to mash the mixture up a bit.

7. Stir in the chopped spinach and vinegar. Press Sauté and let the soup simmer uncovered for 10 minutes more.

8. Serve with chives sprinkled on top of individual servings.

Non-Pantry-Staple Grocery List
- 2 celery ribs
- 4 medium russet potatoes
- 1 teaspoon mustard seeds
- 6 cups chopped spinach
- 1 tablespoon white wine vinegar
- Chopped chives for garnish

Calories 139

Fat 7 g

Fiber 2 g

Carbs 14 g

Net carbs 12 g

Sodium 258 mg

Sugar 4 g

Protein 5 g

Sweet Potato Soup with Kale

Hope Comerford, Clinton Township, MI

Makes 8 servings
Prep. Time: 5 minutes ☙ Cooking Time: 5 minutes ☙ Setting: Manual
Pressure: High ☙ Release: Natural then Manual

1 tablespoon olive oil
1 medium onion, chopped
2 garlic cloves, chopped
2 lb. sweet potatoes, diced
5 cups reduced-sodium chicken stock or vegetable stock
14.5-ounce can diced tomatoes
1 bay leaf
1 teaspoon paprika
½ teaspoon coriander
1 sprig fresh rosemary
¼ teaspoon pepper
5 ounces chopped kale

TIP
You may replace the olive oil with coconut, canola, or grapeseed oil if you wish.

1. Set the Instant Pot to Sauté and heat up the olive oil in the inner pot.

2. Sauté the onion and garlic in the heated oil for 3 to 5 minutes.

3. Press Cancel and add the sweet potatoes, stock, diced tomatoes, bay leaf, paprika, coriander, rosemary, and pepper to the inner pot.

4. Secure the lid and set the vent to sealing.

5. Manually set the Instant Pot to cook for 5 minutes on high pressure.

6. When the cooking time is over, let the pressure release naturally for 10 minutes, then manually release the rest of the pressure.

7. When the pin drops, remove the lid and gently stir the kale into the soup. Let the soup sit for a few minutes so the kale can wilt, then serve.

Non-Pantry-Staple Grocery List
- 2 lb. sweet potatoes
- 14.5-ounce can diced tomatoes
- 1 sprig rosemary
- 5 ounces chopped kale

Calories 195
Fat 4 g
Fiber 5 g
Carbs 34 g
Net carbs 29 g
Sodium 369 mg
Sugar 8 g
Protein 7 g

Sweet Potato Soup with Roasted Red Peppers & Vegetables

Melanie Mohler, Ephrata, PA

Makes 6 servings

Prep. Time: 5 minutes   ❧   Cooking Time: 5 minutes   ❧   Setting: Manual
Pressure: High   ❧   Release: Natural then Manual

2 tablespoons extra-virgin olive oil

1 medium onion, diced

3–4 garlic cloves, minced

2 red bell peppers, halved and seeded

2 medium sweet potatoes, peeled and cubed (about 2 cups)

15-ounce can pinto beans, rinsed and drained

15-ounce can no-salt-added diced tomatoes with herbs

4 cups low-sodium chicken stock or vegetable stock

TIP
You may replace the olive oil with coconut, canola, or grapeseed oil if you wish.

1. Set the Instant Pot to the Sauté function and heat the olive oil in the inner pot.

2. Sauté the onion, garlic, and bell peppers for 5 minutes.

3. Press Cancel and add the sweet potatoes, pinto beans, diced tomatoes, and stock to the inner pot.

4. Secure the lid and manually set the cook time to 5 minutes on high pressure.

5. When the cooking time is over, let the pressure release naturally for 10 minutes, then manually release the rest of the pressure.

6. When the pin drops, remove the lid and use an immersion blender to puree the soup a bit if you like it thicker. If you like it the way it is, leave it, serve, and enjoy!

Non-Pantry-Staple Grocery List
- 2 red bell peppers
- 2 medium sweet potatoes
- 15-ounce can pinto beans
- 15-ounce can no-salt-added diced tomatoes with herbs

Calories 242

Fat 7 g

Fiber 6 g

Carbs 35 g

Net carbs 29 g

Sodium 481 mg

Sugar 9 g

Protein 11 g

Soups, Stews & Chilies   **47**

Flavorful Tomato Soup

Shari Ladd, Hudson, MI

Makes 4 servings
Prep. Time: 10 minutes ❧ Cooking Time: 5 minutes ❧ Setting: Manual
Pressure: High ❧ Release: Natural then Manual

1 tablespoon extra-virgin olive oil

2 tablespoons chopped onion

1 qt. no-salt-added stewed tomatoes

2 teaspoons turbinado sugar or sugar substitute of your choice

½ teaspoon pepper

¼ teaspoon dried basil

½ teaspoon dried oregano

¼ teaspoon dried thyme

6 tablespoons margarine

3 tablespoons flour

2 cups skim milk

Non-Pantry-Staple Grocery List
- 1 qt. no-salt-added stewed tomatoes

1. Set the Instant Pot to Sauté and heat the olive oil.

2. Sauté the onion for 5 minutes in the heated oil in the inner pot.

3. Press Cancel and add the tomatoes, sugar, pepper, basil, oregano, and thyme.

4. Secure the lid and set the vent to sealing.

5. Manually set the cook time for 5 minutes on high pressure.

6. When the cooking time is over, let the pressure release naturally for 15 minutes, then manually release the remaining pressure.

7. While the pressure is releasing, in a small pot on the stove, melt the margarine. Once the margarine is melted, whisk in the flour and cook for 2 minutes, whisking constantly.

8. Slowly whisk the skim milk into the pot.

9. When the pin has dropped next to the pressure valve, remove the lid and slowly whisk the milk/margarine/flour mixture into the tomato soup.

10. Use an immersion blender to puree the soup. Serve and enjoy!

TIP
You may replace the olive oil with canola or grapeseed oil if you wish.

Calories 186
Fat 6 g
Fiber 2 g
Carbs 27 g
Net carbs 25 g
Sodium 1951 mg
Sugar 11 g
Protein 7 g

Creamy Asparagus Soup

Hope Comerford, Clinton Township MI

Makes 4 servings
Prep. Time: 10 minutes & Cooking Time: 5 minutes & Setting: Manual
Pressure: High & Release: Manual

1 lb. asparagus, lower third discarded

1 tablespoon butter

1 medium onion, chopped

1 garlic clove, chopped

5 cups low-sodium chicken stock or vegetable stock

$\frac{1}{2}$ teaspoon salt

$\frac{1}{4}$ teaspoon pepper

$\frac{1}{2}$ cup fat-free heavy cream

1. Chop the asparagus into 1-inch pieces.

2. Set the Instant Pot to Sauté and melt the butter in the inner pot.

3. Sauté the onion, garlic, and asparagus for about 5 minutes.

4. Press Cancel and add the stock, salt, and pepper to the inner pot.

5. Secure the lid and set the vent to sealing.

6. Manually set the cook time to 5 minutes on high pressure.

7. When the cooking time is over, manually release the pressure.

8. When the pin drops, remove the lid. Use an immersion blender to puree the soup.

9. *Very* slowly, whisk the heavy cream into the soup. Serve and enjoy!

Non-Pantry-Staple Grocery List
- 1 lb. asparagus
- $\frac{1}{2}$ cup fat-free heavy cream

Calories 186
Fat 7 g
Fiber 3 g
Carbs 20 g
Net carbs 17 g
Sodium 697 mg
Sugar 9 g
Protein 11 g

Lighter Cream of Broccoli Soup

Hope Comerford, Clinton Township, MI

Makes 4 servings
Prep. Time: 10 minutes ❧ Cooking Time: 5 minutes ❧ Setting: Sauté and Manual
Pressure: High ❧ Release: Manual

2 tablespoons butter or margarine

1 medium onion, chopped

2 garlic cloves, chopped

1 lb. (about 5 cups) chopped fresh broccoli

4 cups low-sodium chicken, or vegetable stock

½ teaspoon salt

¼ teaspoon pepper

2 tablespoons cornstarch

1 cup fat-free heavy cream, *divided*

½ cup low-fat shredded cheddar cheese

1. Set the Instant Pot to Sauté and melt the butter.

2. When the butter is melted, sauté the onion and garlic for 5 minutes.

3. Press Cancel and add the broccoli, stock, salt, and pepper.

4. Secure the lid and set the vent to sealing.

5. Manually set the cook time to 5 minutes on high pressure.

6. When the cooking time is over, manually release the pressure.

7. When the pin drops, remove the lid and use a potato smasher to break up the broccoli a bit and thicken the soup.

8. In a small dish, mix the cornstarch with a bit of the heavy cream until smooth. Then, whisk the cornstarch/heavy cream with the remaining heavy cream and *slowly* whisk this mixture into the soup.

9. Serve each bowl with a sprinkle of shredded cheddar cheese and enjoy!

Non-Pantry-Staple Grocery List
- 5 cups (1 lb.) chopped broccoli
- 1 cup fat-free heavy cream
- ½ cup low-fat shredded cheddar cheese

Calories 265
Fat 11 g
Fiber 3 g
Carbs 28 g
Net carbs 25 g
Sodium 827 mg
Sugar 10 g
Protein 15 g

Curried Carrot Bisque

Kathy Stoltzfus, Leola, PA

Makes 6 servings
Prep. Time: 2 minutes ⚮ Cooking Time: 15 minutes ⚮ Setting: Manual
Pressure: High ⚮ Release: Natural

8 medium carrots, peeled and chopped

1 onion, chopped

1 tart apple, peeled and chopped

1 teaspoon curry powder

1 garlic clove, crushed

¼ teaspoon ground coriander

¼ teaspoon salt

⅛ teaspoon allspice

3 cups low-sodium chicken, or vegetable stock

14-ounce can low-fat coconut milk

Chopped fresh cilantro

1. Place all ingredients except the chopped fresh cilantro into the inner pot of the Instant Pot and secure the lid. Make sure the vent is set to sealing.

2. Manually set the cook time for 15 minutes on high pressure.

3. When the cooking time is over, let the pressure release naturally.

4. When the pin drops, remove the lid and use an immersion blender to puree the bisque.

5. When serving, top each bowl with a sprinkle of fresh cilantro.

Non-Pantry-Staple Grocery List
- 8 medium carrots
- 1 tart apple
- 1 teaspoon curry powder
- ⅛ teaspoon allspice
- 14-ounce can low-fat coconut milk
- Small amount fresh cilantro

Calories 141
Fat 5 g
Fiber 3 g
Carbs 20 g
Net carbs 17 g
Sodium 241 mg
Sugar 10 g
Protein 5 g

Garden Vegetable Soup with Pasta

Jan McDowell, New Holland, PA

Makes 6 servings ❧ *Prep. Time: 5 minutes* ❧ *Cooking Time: 5 minutes*
Setting: Manual ❧ *Pressure: High* ❧ *Release: Manual*

1 tablespoon olive oil
1 chopped onion
1 teaspoon chopped garlic
1 small zucchini, chopped
½ lb. fresh mushrooms, sliced or chopped
1 bell pepper, chopped
24-ounce can no-salt-added tomatoes
1 tablespoon fresh basil
4 cups low-sodium vegetable stock
1 cup water
¾ cup whole-grain small shell noodles
Dash hot sauce, *optional*

1. Set the Instant Pot to Sauté and heat the olive oil in the inner pot.

2. Sauté the onion and garlic for 5 minutes.

3. Press Cancel and add the zucchini, mushrooms, bell pepper, tomatoes, basil, vegetable stock, and water to the inner pot. Pour in the noodles, but *do not stir*, just push them gently under the liquid.

4. Secure the lid and make sure the vent is set to sealing.

5. Manually set the cook time to 5 minutes on high pressure.

6. When the cooking time is over, manually release the pressure.

7. Serve each bowl with a dash of optional hot sauce and enjoy!

TIP
You may replace the olive oil with canola or grapeseed oil if you wish.

Non-Pantry-Staple Grocery List
- 1 small zucchini
- ½ lb. mushrooms
- 1 bell pepper
- 24-ounce can tomatoes
- 1 tablespoon fresh basil
- ¾ cup whole-grain small shell noodles
- Dash hot sauce, *optional*

Calories 97
Fat 3 g
Fiber 5 g
Carbs 17 g
Net carbs 12 g
Sodium 161 mg
Sugar 5 g
Protein 4 g

Zesty Pumpkin Soup

Miriam Christophel, Goshen, IN

Makes 6 servings
Prep. Time: 5 minutes   ⚘   Cooking Time: 8 minutes   ⚘   Setting: Sauté and Manual
Pressure: High   ⚘   Release: Manual

2 tablespoons olive oil

1 cup chopped onions

1 garlic clove, crushed

3 cups low-sodium chicken stock or vegetable stock

15-ounce can pure pumpkin puree

1 teaspoon curry powder

$\frac{1}{2}$ teaspoon salt

$\frac{1}{8}$–$\frac{1}{4}$ teaspoon ground coriander

$\frac{1}{8}$ teaspoon crushed red pepper

1 cup fat-free half-and-half

Chopped chives as garnish, *optional*

TIP
You may replace the olive oil with canola or grapeseed oil if you wish.

1. Set the Instant Pot to the Sauté function and heat the olive oil in the inner pot.

2. Sauté the onions and garlic for 5 minutes.

3. Press Cancel and add the stock, pumpkin puree, curry powder, salt, coriander, and crushed red pepper to the inner pot. Stir to combine.

4. Secure the lid and set the vent to sealing.

5. Manually set the cook time for 8 minutes on high pressure.

6. When cook time is done, manually release the pressure and open the lid when the pin drops.

7. Use an immersion blender to puree the soup, then *slowly* whisk in the half-and-half.

8. Serve each bowl with a sprinkle of chives, if using.

Non-Pantry-Staple Grocery List
- 15-ounce can pumpkin puree
- 1 teaspoon curry powder
- $\frac{1}{8}$ teaspoon crushed red pepper
- 1 cup fat-free half-and-half
- Small amount chopped chives

Calories 143
Fat 7 g
Fiber 3 g
Carbs 16 g
Net carbs 63 g
Sodium 376 mg
Sugar 7 g
Protein 5 g

Veggie Minestrone

Dorothy VanDeest, Memphis, TN

Makes 8 servings
Prep. Time: 5 minutes ❧ Cooking Time: 4 minutes ❧ Setting: Sauté and Manual
Pressure: High ❧ Release: Manual

2 tablespoons olive oil

1 large onion, chopped

1 garlic clove, minced

4 cups low-sodium chicken, or vegetable stock

16-ounce can kidney beans, rinsed and drained

14.5-ounce can no-salt-added diced tomatoes

2 medium carrots, sliced thin

¼ teaspoon dried oregano

¼ teaspoon pepper

½ cup whole wheat elbow macaroni, uncooked

4 ounces fresh spinach

½ cup grated Parmesan cheese

TIP
You may replace the olive oil with canola or grapeseed oil if you wish.

1. Set the Instant Pot to the Sauté function and heat the olive oil.

2. When the olive oil is heated, add the onion and garlic to the inner pot and sauté for 5 minutes.

3. Press Cancel and add the stock, kidney beans, tomatoes, carrots, oregano, and pepper. Gently pour in the macaroni, but *do not stir*. Just push the noodles gently under the liquid.

4. Secure the lid and set the vent to sealing.

5. Manually set the cook time for 4 minutes on high pressure.

6. When the cooking time is over, manually release the pressure and remove the lid when the pin drops.

7. Stir in the spinach and let wilt a few minutes.

8. Sprinkle 1 tablespoon grated Parmesan on each individual bowl of this soup. Enjoy!

Non-Pantry-Staple Grocery List
- 16-ounce can low-sodium kidney beans
- 14.5-ounce can no-salt-added diced tomatoes
- 2 medium carrots
- ½ cup whole wheat elbow macaroni
- 4 ounces fresh spinach
- ½ cup grated Parmesan cheese

Calories 238
Fat 6 g
Fiber 8 g
Carbs 35 g
Net carbs 27 g
Sodium 550 mg
Sugar 6 g
Protein 12 g

Sausage, Beans, and Rice Soup

Sharon Easter, Yuba City, CA

Makes 5 servings
Prep. Time: 5–8 minutes ❧ *Cooking Time: 20 minutes* ❧ *Setting: Manual*
Pressure: High ❧ *Release: Natural then Manual*

1 tablespoon olive oil

½ lb. bulk turkey sausage

28-ounce can no-salt-added diced tomatoes

¼ teaspoon pepper

½ teaspoon dried oregano

½ cup uncooked brown rice

15-ounce can cannellini beans, rinsed and drained

6 cups low-sodium chicken stock or vegetable stock

1. Set the Instant Pot to Sauté and heat the olive oil in the inner pot.

2. Sauté the turkey sausage for 5 minutes, or until lightly browned.

3. Press Cancel and then add the tomatoes, pepper, oregano, brown rice, beans, and stock to the inner pot.

4. Secure the lid and set the vent to sealing.

5. Manually set the time for 20 minutes on high pressure.

6. When the cooking time is over, let the pressure release naturally for 10 minutes, then manually release the remaining pressure.

7. Serve and enjoy!

TIP
You may replace the olive oil with canola or grapeseed oil if you wish.

Non-Pantry-Staple Grocery List
- ½ lb. bulk turkey sausage
- 15-ounce can cannellini beans

Calories 438

Fat 13 g

Fiber 7 g

Carbs 52 g

Net carbs 45 g

Sodium 1016 mg

Sugar 9 g

Protein 26 g

Turkey Peasant Soup

Alice Valine, Elma, NY

Makes 8 servings
Prep. Time: 11 minutes ⚜ Cooking Time: 5 minutes ⚜ Setting: Sauté and Manual
Pressure: High ⚜ Release: Natural then Manual

2 tablespoons olive oil

1 medium onion, chopped

2–3 garlic cloves, minced

½ lb. bulk turkey sausage

2 (15-ounce) cans cannellini beans, rinsed and drained

2 (14.5-ounce) cans no-salt-added diced tomatoes

4 cups low-sodium chicken stock or vegetable stock

2 teaspoons Italian seasoning

3 medium zucchini, sliced

4 cups fresh spinach leaves, chopped, or baby spinach, un-chopped

Shredded Parmesan or Romano, cheese, *optional*

1. Set the Instant Pot to Sauté and heat the olive oil in the inner pot.

2. Sauté the onion and garlic for about 3 minutes. Push it to the outer edges and brown the turkey sausage for an additional 5 to 8 minutes.

3. Press Cancel and add the beans, tomatoes, chicken stock, Italian seasoning, and zucchini.

4. Secure the lid and set the vent to sealing.

5. Manually set the cook time for 5 minutes on high pressure.

6. When the cooking time is over, let the pressure release naturally for 10 minutes, then manually release the remaining pressure.

7. When the pin drops, remove the lid and stir in the spinach. Allow the spinach to wilt.

8. Serve each bowl with an optional sprinkle of shredded cheese.

Non-Pantry-Staple Grocery List
- ½ lb. bulk turkey sausage
- 2 (15-ounce) cans cannellini beans
- 2 (14.5-ounce) cans no-salt-added diced tomatoes
- 2 teaspoons Italian seasoning
- 3 medium zucchini
- 4 cups fresh spinach or baby spinach
- Shredded Parmesan or Romano cheese, *optional*

Calories 266
Fat 8 g
Fiber 7 g
Carbs 32 g
Net carbs 25 g
Sodium 311 mg
Sugar 4 g
Protein 17 g

TIP
You may replace the olive oil with canola or grapeseed oil if you wish.

Lentil Barley Stew with Chicken

Ilene Bontrager, Arlington, KS

Makes 4 servings
Prep. Time: 8–11 minutes   ♣   Cooking Time: 18 minutes   ♣   Setting: Manual
Pressure: High   ♣   Release: Natural

2 tablespoons olive oil

½ onion, chopped

1 small celery rib, sliced thin

1 carrot, cut in fine dice

½ lb. boneless, skinless chicken breast, chopped

⅓ cup uncooked lentils, rinsed

⅓ cup uncooked green split peas

⅓ cup uncooked pearl barley

¼ teaspoon pepper

6 cups low-sodium chicken stock

1. Set the Instant Pot to Sauté and heat the olive oil.

2. Sauté the onion, celery, and carrot for about 3 minutes, then add the chopped chicken. Continue cooking an additional 5 to 8 minutes or until the chicken is browned.

3. Press Cancel and add the lentils, split peas, pearl barley, pepper, and chicken stock.

4. Secure the lid and set the vent to sealing.

5. Manually set the cook time to 18 minutes on high pressure.

6. When the cooking time is over, let the pressure release naturally.

TIP
You may replace the olive oil with canola or grapeseed oil if you wish.

Non-Pantry-Staple Grocery List
- 1 celery rib
- 1 carrot
- ½ lb. boneless, skinless chicken breast
- ⅓ cup lentils
- ⅓ cup green split peas
- ⅓ cup pearl barley

Calories 162

Fat 5 g

Fiber 3 g

Carbs 24 g

Net carbs 21 g

Sodium 353 mg

Sugar 4 g

Protein 6 g

Turkey Sausage and Cabbage Soup

Hope Comerford, Clinton Township, MI

Makes 8 servings

Prep. Time: 5 minutes ❧ Cooking Time: 17 minutes ❧ Setting: Sauté and Manual
Pressure: High ❧ Release: Manual

2 tablespoons olive oil

1½ cups chopped onions

2 garlic cloves, finely chopped

3 carrots, chopped in rounds

1 lb. bulk Italian turkey sausage, removed from casing

1 medium head green cabbage, shredded

2 (14.5-ounce) cans no-salt-added diced tomatoes

1 tablespoon dried basil

2 teaspoons dried oregano

¼ teaspoon black pepper

32 ounces low-sodium chicken stock or vegetable stock

1. Set the Instant Pot to Sauté and heat the olive oil in the inner pot.

2. Sauté the onions, garlic, and carrots for 2 minutes, then push them to the outer edges and add the sausage. Brown the sausage for about 3 minutes. Press Cancel.

3. Add the cabbage, tomatoes, basil, oregano, and black pepper. Finally, pour in the stock.

4. Secure the lid and set the vent to sealing.

5. Manually cook for 17 minutes on high pressure.

6. When the cooking time is over, manually release the pressure. Serve and enjoy!

TIP
You may replace the olive oil with canola or grapeseed oil if you wish.

Non-Pantry-Staple Grocery List
- 3 carrots
- 1 lb. bulk Italian turkey sausage
- 1 medium head green cabbage
- 2 (14.5-ounce) cans no-salt-added diced tomatoes

Calories 207
Fat 11 g
Fiber 2 g
Carbs 14 g
Net carbs 12 g
Sodium 1173 mg
Sugar 5 g
Protein 12 g

Chicken Noodle Soup

Hope Comerford, Clinton Township, MI

Makes 7 servings
Prep. Time: 10 minutes ☙ Cooking Time: 30 minutes ☙ Setting: Manual then Keep Warm
Pressure: High ☙ Release: Manual

2 lb. whole chicken, skin removed

3 medium carrots, sliced

1 large onion, skin removed, but left whole

½ teaspoon pepper

1 bay leaf

1 teaspoon oregano

½ teaspoon basil

2 teaspoons salt

32 ounces low-sodium chicken stock

6 cups water (or enough to just reach the fill line)

8 ounces uncooked pasta of your choice

TIP

If you plan to have leftovers, you may consider skipping step 7. Instead, you can cook your noodles on the stove, then place the desired amount of cooked noodles in each bowl and spoon the chicken soup over the noodles for each serving.

1. Place the chicken, carrots, onion, pepper, bay leaf, oregano, basil, salt, chicken stock, and water (enough to fill the inner pot to the fill line) in the inner pot of the Instant Pot.

2. Secure the lid and set the vent to sealing.

3. Set the cook time manually to 30 minutes on high pressure.

4. When the cooking time is over, manually release the pressure.

5. Remove and discard the onion and bay leaf.

6. Carefully remove the chicken from the pot and remove the meat from the bones, discarding the bones. Shred the meat as best you can and place back in inner pot.

7. Add the noodles of your choice, secure the lid back on, and turn the Instant Pot to Keep Warm. Let the noodles cook for about 15 minutes. If you are using noodles that have a fast cook time, check on them sooner.

Non-Pantry-Staple Grocery List
- 2 lb. whole chicken, skinless
- 3 medium carrots
- 8 ounces uncooked pasta of your choice

Calories 303

Fat 5 g

Fiber 2 g

Carbs 28 g

Net carbs 26 g

Sodium 1022 mg

Sugar 3 g

Protein 36 g

Soups, Stews & Chilies 63

Chicken Barley Soup

Ida H. Goering, Dayton, VA

Makes 6 servings
Prep. Time: 8–11 minutes ❧ Cooking Time: 18 minutes ❧ Setting: Sauté and Manual
Pressure: High ❧ Release: Natural

2 tablespoons olive oil

2½ medium carrots, diced

3 celery ribs, diced

1 small onion, chopped

1 lb. boneless, skinless chicken, chopped

¾ cup uncooked pearl barley

14.5-ounce can no-salt-added diced tomatoes

½ teaspoon black pepper

1 bay leaf

6 cups low-sodium chicken stock

2 tablespoons chopped fresh parsley

1. Set the Instant Pot to Sauté and heat the olive oil.

2. When the oil is heated, sauté the carrots, celery, and onion for about 3 minutes, then add the chicken and sauté for an additional 5 to 8 minutes, or until lightly browned.

3. Press Cancel and add the pearl barley, tomatoes, pepper, bay leaf, and chicken stock to the inner pot.

4. Secure the lid and set the vent to sealing.

5. Manually set the time for 18 minutes on high pressure.

6. When the cooking time is over, let the pressure release naturally.

7. Serve this with a sprinkle of fresh chopped parsley in each bowl.

TIP
You may replace the olive oil with canola or grapeseed oil if you wish.

Non-Pantry-Staple Grocery List
- 2½ carrots
- 3 celery ribs
- 1 lb. boneless, skinless chicken breast
- ¾ cup pearl barley
- 14.5-ounce can no-salt-added diced tomatoes
- 2 tablespoons fresh chopped parsley

Calories 323

Fat 9 g

Fiber 5 g

Carbs 34 g

Net carbs 29 g

Sodium 518 mg

Sugar 7 g

Protein 27 g

Spicy Chicken Soup with Edamame

J. B. Miller, Indianapolis, IN

Makes 8 servings

Prep. Time: 8 minutes ❧ Cooking Time: 20 minutes ❧ Setting: Sauté, Manual, Keep Warm
Pressure: High ❧ Release: Manual

2 tablespoons olive oil

1 bunch (about 6) scallions, thinly sliced

1 red bell pepper, chopped

1 yellow bell pepper, chopped

2 jalapeño peppers, seeded and finely chopped

4 garlic cloves, chopped

1½ lb. boneless, skinless, chicken breasts

½ teaspoon ground ginger

½ teaspoon ground pepper

4 cups low-sodium chicken broth

3 cups fresh, or frozen, edamame, shelled

TIP

You may replace the olive oil with canola or grapeseed oil if you wish.

1. Set the Instant Pot to Sauté and heat up the oil in the inner pot.

2. Sauté the scallions, bell peppers, jalapeños, and garlic in the oil for about 3 minutes. Push them to the outer edges and sear the chicken breasts on both sides.

3. Press Cancel. Add the remaining ingredients, except for the edamame, and secure the lid. Make sure the vent is set to sealing.

4. Manually set the cook time for 15 minutes on high pressure.

5. When the cooking time is over, manually release the pressure.

6. When the pin drops, remove the lid, then remove the chicken and shred it between 2 forks. Replace it back in the soup.

7. Stir the edamame into the soup and press Keep Warm. Allow it to cook for about 5 additional minutes, then serve.

Non-Pantry-Staple Grocery List
- 1 bunch scallions
- 1 red bell pepper
- 1 yellow bell pepper
- 2 jalapeño peppers
- 1½ lb. boneless, skinless chicken breasts
- ½ teaspoon ground ginger
- 3 cups fresh or frozen shelled edamame

Calories 319
Fat 12 g
Fiber 4 g
Carbs 13 g
Net carbs 9 g
Sodium 245 mg
Sugar 4 g
Protein 36 g

Chicken Chili Pepper Stew

Susan Kasting, Jenks, OK

Makes 4 servings
Prep. Time: 5 minutes ⚬ *Cooking Time: 8 minutes* ⚬ *Setting: Manual*
Pressure: High ⚬ *Release: Natural then Manual*

14.5 ounces low-sodium chicken stock

1 lb. boneless, skinless chicken breasts,

4 garlic cloves, minced

1–2 jalapeño peppers, seeded and diced

1 medium red bell pepper, diced

1 medium carrot, sliced

15-ounce can no-salt-added corn, drained

1 teaspoon cumin

2 tablespoons chopped cilantro

1. Place all of the ingredients, except the chopped cilantro, into the inner pot of the Instant Pot and secure the lid. Set the vent to sealing.

2. Manually set the cook time for 8 minutes on high pressure.

3. When the cooking time is over, let the pressure release naturally for 5 minutes, then manually release the pressure.

4. When the pin drops, remove the lid, remove the chicken, shred between 2 forks, then replace back in the inner pot. Stir.

5. Serve each bowl of stew with a sprinkling of chopped cilantro.

Non-Pantry-Staple Grocery List
- 1 lb. boneless, skinless chicken breasts
- 1–2 jalapeño peppers
- 1 medium red bell pepper
- 1 medium carrot
- 15-ounce can no-salt-added corn
- 2 tablespoons chopped cilantro

Calories 258

Fat 4 g

Fiber 5 g

Carbs 26 g

Net carbs 21 g

Sodium 156 mg

Sugar 13 g

Protein 30 g

Hearty Vegetable Soup

Berenice M. Wagner, Dodge City, KS
Sherri Grindle, Goshen, IN

Makes 8 servings
Prep. Time: 8–10 minutes ⚜ Cooking Time: 17 minutes ⚜ Setting: Sauté and Manual
Pressure: High ⚜ Release: Natural then Manual

½ lb. 95% lean ground beef or ground turkey

1 medium onion, chopped

1 garlic clove, minced

2 carrots, sliced

14.5-ounce can no-salt-added diced tomatoes

¾ cup uncooked quick-cooking barley

2 low-sodium beef bouillon cubes

½ teaspoon dried basil

1 bay leaf

6 cups water

9-ounce package frozen mixed vegetables

1. Set the Instant Pot to Sauté and brown the ground beef, onion, and garlic in the inner pot.

2. Press Cancel. Add the carrots, tomatoes with their juices, barley, bouillon, basil, bay leaf, and water.

3. Secure the lid and set the vent to sealing.

4. Manually set the cook time for 7 minutes on high pressure.

5. When the cooking time is over, let the pressure release naturally for 15 minutes, then manually release the remaining pressure.

6. When the pin drops, remove the lid and stir in the frozen mixed vegetables. Let them sit in the soup about 10 minutes.

7. Serve and enjoy!

Non-Pantry-Staple Grocery List
- ½ lb. 95% lean ground beef
- 2 carrots
- 14.5-ounce can no-salt-added diced tomatoes
- ¾ cup quick-cooking barley
- 2 low-sodium beef bouillon cubes
- 9-ounce package frozen mixed vegetables

Calories 191

Fat 8 g

Fiber 5 g

Carbs 23 g

Net carbs 3 g

Sodium 523 mg

Sugar 3 g

Protein 8 g

TIP
If you decide to use ground turkey, you will need to add 1 tablespoon olive oil (or oil of your choice) to the pot before browning.

Soups, Stews & Chilies 69

Stuffed Sweet Pepper Soup

Moreen Weaver, Bath, NY

Makes 10 servings
Prep. Time: 10 minutes ⚘ Cooking Time: 10 minutes ⚘ Setting: Sauté then Manual
Pressure: High ⚘ Release: Natural then Manual

1 lb. 95% lean ground beef

¼ teaspoon salt

⅛ teaspoon pepper

2 garlic cloves, minced

1 large onion, diced

2 quarts low-sodium tomato juice, *divided*

3 medium red, or green, bell peppers, diced

1½ cups chili sauce, no-salt-added

1 cup uncooked brown rice

2 celery ribs, diced

3 low-sodium chicken bouillon cubes

1. Set the Instant Pot to the Sauté function and cook the ground beef with salt, pepper, onion, and garlic until the beef is no longer pink.

2. Pour in a small amount (about ½ cup) of tomato juice and scrape the bottom of the inner pot.

3. Press Cancel. Add all of the remaining ingredients. Secure the lid and set the vent to sealing.

4. Manually set the cook time for 10 minutes on high pressure.

5. When the cooking time is over, let the pressure release naturally for 5 minutes, then manually release any remaining pressure. Serve and enjoy.

Non-Pantry-Staple Grocery List
- 1 lb. 95% lean ground beef
- 2 qts. low-sodium tomato juice
- 3 medium bell peppers (red or green)
- 1½ cups no-salt-added chili sauce
- 2 celery ribs
- 3 low-sodium chicken bouillon cubes

Calories 217
Fat 4 g
Fiber 4 g
Carbs 32 g
Net carbs 28 g
Sodium 1228 mg
Sugar 11 g
Protein 14 g

Beef Mushroom Barley Soup

Becky Frey, Lebanon, PA

Makes 8 servings
Prep. Time: 20 minutes ❧ Cooking Time: 25 minutes ❧ Setting: Sauté then Manual
Pressure: High ❧ Release: Natural then Manual

2 tablespoons olive oil, *divided*
1 lb. boneless beef chuck, cubed
1 large onion, chopped
2 garlic cloves, crushed
1 lb. fresh mushrooms, sliced
1 celery rib, sliced
2 carrots, sliced
½ teaspoon dried thyme, *optional*
8 cups low-sodium beef stock
½ cup uncooked pearl barley
½ teaspoon freshly ground pepper
3 tablespoons chopped fresh parsley

1. Set the Instant Pot to the Sauté function and heat up 1 tablespoon of the olive oil in the inner pot.

2. Brown the beef, in batches if needed, and then remove and set aside.

3. Add the remaining tablespoon of olive oil and sauté the onion, garlic, and mushrooms for 3 to 4 minutes.

4. Add the beef back in, as well as all of the remaining ingredients, except for the parsley. Press Cancel.

5. Secure the lid and set the vent to sealing.

6. Manually set the cook time to 25 minutes on high pressure.

7. When the cooking time is over, let the pressure release naturally for 15 minutes, then manually release the remaining pressure.

8. When the pin drops, remove the lid and stir. Serve each bowl topped with some fresh chopped parsley.

Non-Pantry-Staple Grocery List
- 1 lb. cubed boneless beef chuck
- 1 lb. fresh sliced mushrooms
- 1 celery rib
- 2 carrots
- ½ cup pearl barley
- 3 tablespoons fresh chopped parsley

Calories 243
Fat 12 g
Fiber 3 g
Carbs 16 g
Net carbs 13 g
Sodium 539 mg
Sugar 4 g
Protein 19 g

Beef and Black Bean Chili

Eileen B. Jarvis, St. Augustine, FL

Makes 8 servings

Prep. Time:10 minutes ❧ Cooking Time: 20 minutes ❧ Setting: Chili/Beans ❧ Release: Manual

1 teaspoon olive oil

1 lb. 95% lean ground beef

1 small onion, chopped

2 (15-ounce) cans no-salt-added black beans, rinsed and drained

¾ cup water or reduced-sodium beef stock

1 cup medium, or hot, chunky salsa

16-ounce can no-salt-added tomato sauce

1 tablespoon chili powder

Low-fat sour cream, *optional*

Shredded reduced-fat cheddar cheese, *optional*

TIP
You may replace the olive oil with canola or grapeseed oil if you wish.

1. Set the Instant Pot to Sauté and heat the oil in the inner pot.

2. Brown the beef until no longer pink along with the onion.

3. Press Cancel. Add the remaining ingredients except for the sour cream and shredded cheese, then secure the lid. Set the vent to sealing.

4. Set the Instant Pot to Chili/Beans and set the cook time for 20 minutes.

5. When the cooking time is over, release the pressure manually.

6. When serving, if you wish, top individual servings with sour cream and/or a sprinkle of shredded reduced-fat cheddar cheese.

Non-Pantry-Staple Grocery List
- 1 lb. 95% lean ground beef
- 2 (15-ounce) cans no-salt-added black beans
- ¾ cup reduced-sodium beef stock or water
- 1 cup salsa of your choice
- 16-ounce can no-salt-added tomato sauce
- Low-fat sour cream, *optional*
- Shredded reduced-fat cheddar cheese, *optional*

Calories 279

Fat 5 g

Fiber 11 g

Carbs 34 g

Net carbs 23 g

Sodium 700 mg

Sugar 5 g

Protein 24 g

Tomato Beef Soup

Hope Comerford, Clinton Township, MI

Makes 6 servings
Prep. Time: 10 minutes ⚜ Cooking Time: 8 minutes ⚜ Setting: Manual
Pressure: High ⚜ Release: Manual

1 teaspoon olive oil

1 lb. 95% lean ground beef

½ teaspoon salt

⅛ teaspoon black pepper

1 small onion, chopped

2 garlic cloves, chopped

4 cups reduced-sodium beef stock, *divided*

2 tablespoon tomato paste

2 (14.5-ounce) cans reduced-sodium diced tomatoes

2 carrots, sliced

1 chopped green, or red, bell pepper

1 large potato, diced

1 teaspoon Italian seasoning, *optional*

1. Set the Instant Pot to Sauté and heat the teaspoon of olive oil in the inner pot.

2. Brown the ground beef with salt, pepper, onion, and garlic, until the beef is no longer pink.

3. Pour in about ½ cup of beef stock into the bottom of the inner pot and scrape. Then, add the remaining ingredients to the inner pot. Press Cancel.

4. Secure the lid and set the vent to sealing.

5. Manually set the time for 8 minutes on high pressure.

6. When the cooking time is over, release the pressure manually. Serve and enjoy!

TIP
You may replace the olive oil with canola or grapeseed oil if you wish.

Non-Pantry-Staple Grocery List
- 1 lb. 95% lean ground beef
- 4 cups low-sodium beef stock
- 2 tablespoons tomato paste
- 2 (14.5-ounce) cans diced tomatoes
- 2 carrots
- 1 green or red bell pepper
- 1 large potato
- 1 teaspoon Italian seasoning

Calories 260

Fat 8 g

Fiber 5 g

Carbs 37 g

Net carbs 32 g

Sodium 582 mg

Sugar 6 g

Protein 10 g

Ham and Bean Soup

Susie Nisley, Millersburg, OH

Makes 10 servings
Prep. Time: 6 minutes ⚜ Cooking Time: 30 minutes ⚜ Setting: Manual
Pressure: High ⚜ Release: Natural then Manual

1 tablespoon olive oil
1 small onion, chopped
1 green bell pepper, diced
$\frac{1}{2}$ carrot, diced
1 lb. extra-lean ham, diced
1 lb. dry navy beans, rinsed
1 cup no-salt-added tomato juice
7 cups reduced-sodium chicken stock
2 teaspoons garlic powder
$\frac{1}{2}$ teaspoon cumin
$\frac{1}{2}$ teaspoon black pepper
1 teaspoon no-salt seasoning
1 bunch fresh cilantro, chopped

1. Set the Instant Pot to Sauté and heat up the oil.

2. Sauté the onion, bell pepper, and carrot for 3 minutes. Add the ham and sauté an additional 3 minutes.

3. Press Cancel. Place all remaining ingredients except the cilantro into the inner pot and secure the lid. Set the vent to sealing.

4. Manually set the Instant Pot to cook for 30 minutes on high pressure.

5. When the cooking time is over, let the pressure release naturally for 10 minutes, then manually release the remaining pressure.

6. Before serving, stir in the chopped fresh cilantro.

TIP
You may replace the olive oil with canola or grapeseed oil if you wish.

Non-Pantry-Staple Grocery List
- 1 green bell pepper
- $\frac{1}{2}$ carrot
- 1 lb. extra-lean ham
- 1 lb. navy beans
- 1 cup no-salt-added tomato juice
- 1 teaspoon no-salt seasoning
- 1 bunch fresh cilantro

Calories 301
Fat 7 g
Fiber 7 g
Carbs 37 g
Net carbs 30 g
Sodium 834 mg
Sugar 6 g
Protein 24 g

Senate Bean Soup

Dorothea Ladd, Ballston Lake, NY

Makes 8 servings
Prep. Time: 5 minutes ⚶ Cooking Time: 5 minutes ⚶ Setting: Manual
Pressure: High ⚶ Release: Manual

1 tablespoon olive oil

2 garlic cloves, minced

1 large onion, diced

1½ cups diced lean ham

2 large carrots, sliced

2 celery ribs, sliced

2 (15-ounce) cans cannellini beans, or great northern beans, rinsed and drained

1 tablespoon dried parsley

1 pinch sage

8 cups low-sodium chicken stock (or less)

1. Set the Instant Pot to Sauté and add the oil to heat up in the inner pot.

2. Sauté the garlic, onion, and ham for about 5 minutes.

3. Press Cancel. Add all of the remaining ingredients, being mindful of how much chicken stock you add depending on how thin or thick you prefer your soup.

4. Secure the lid and set the vent to sealing.

5. Manually set the cook time for 5 minutes on high pressure.

6. When the cooking time is over, manually release the pressure. Serve and enjoy.

TIP

You may replace the olive oil with canola or grapeseed oil if you wish.

Non-Pantry-Staple Grocery List
- 1½ cups diced lean ham
- 2 large carrots
- 2 celery ribs
- 2 (15-ounce) cans cannellini beans or great northern beans
- 1 tablespoon dried parsley
- Pinch sage

Calories 262

Fat 6 g

Fiber 6 g

Carbs 34 g

Net carbs 28 g

Sodium 1059 mg

Sugar 5 g

Protein 19 g

Soups, Stews & Chilies ⚶ **77**

Napa Cabbage and Pork Soup

Shirley Unternahrer, Wayland, IA

Makes 8 servings
Prep. Time: 7 minutes ❧ Cooking Time: 18 minutes ❧ Setting: Sauté then Manual
Pressure: High ❧ Release: Manual

I teaspoon olive oil

I small onion, chopped

I lb. lean ground pork* (not sausage)

4 cups low sodium chicken stock

2 tablespoons fish sauce (found in Asian foods section)

½ teaspoon turbinado sugar, or sugar of your choice

I head (about 8 cups) napa cabbage, shredded

6 scallions, chopped

TIP

You may replace the olive oil with canola or grapeseed oil if you wish.

1. Set the Instant Pot to the Sauté function and add the olive oil to heat.

2. Sauté the onion for 2 minutes, then place the ground pork into the inner pot and brown it for about 5 minutes.

3. Press Cancel. Pour in the chicken stock, fish sauce, sugar, and cabbage, then secure the lid. Set the vent to sealing.

4. Manually set the cook time for 18 minutes on high pressure.

5. When the cooking time is over, manually release the pressure.

6. When serving, top each bowl with a sprinkling of scallions.

Non-Pantry-Staple Grocery List
- I lb. lean ground pork
- 2 tablespoons fish sauce
- I head napa cabbage
- 6 scallions

Calories 241
Fat 17 g
Fiber 1 g
Carbs 10 g
Net carbs 9 g
Sodium 817 mg
Sugar 4 g
Protein 13 g

Soups, Stews & Chilies ❧ **79**

Green Bean and Ham Soup

Carla Keslowsky, Hillsboro, KS

Makes 4 servings

Prep. Time: 4–5 minutes ❧ Cooking Time: 24 minutes ❧ Setting: Sauté and Manual
Pressure: High ❧ Release: Natural and Manual

1 teaspoon olive oil

1 medium onion, chopped

1 ham hock

7½ cups water or reduced-sodium chicken stock

2 potatoes, peeled and cubed

1 sprig fresh dill weed

16-ounce package frozen no-salt-added green beans or 1 lb. fresh beans

½ teaspoon black pepper

½ cup fat-free milk

Non-Pantry-Staple Grocery List
- 1 ham hock
- 2 potatoes
- 1 sprig fresh dill
- 16 ounces frozen no-salt-added green beans or 1 lb. fresh green beans

1. Using the Sauté function on the Instant Pot, heat the oil in the inner pot. Sauté the onion for 4 to 5 minutes.

2. Press Cancel, then add the ham hock and water.

3. Secure the lid and set the vent to sealing.

4. Manually set the cook time for 20 minutes on high pressure.

5. When the cooking time is over, let the pressure release naturally for 10 minutes, then manually release the remaining pressure.

6. Add the remaining ingredients, except for the milk, and secure the lid. Set the vent to sealing.

7. Set the Instant Pot to cook manually for 4 minutes on high pressure.

8. When the cooking time is over, manually release the pressure.

9. When the pin drops, remove the lid. Remove the ham hock and separate the meat from the bone. Discard the bone and stir the ham meat back into the soup.

10. Slowly stir in the milk. Let it heat through and serve.

Calories 303
Fat 8 g
Fiber 6 g
Carbs 36 g
Net carbs 30 g
Sodium 1698 mg
Sugar 14 g
Protein 23 g

TIP
You may replace the olive oil with canola or grapeseed oil if you wish.

Main Dishes

Delectable Eggplant

Thelma Good, Harrisonburg, VA

Makes 3 main-dish servings
Prep. Time: 20 minutes ✤ Cooking Time: 10 minutes ✤ Cooling Time: 10 minutes
Setting: Manual ✤ Pressure: High ✤ Release: Manual

2 teaspoons olive oil

½ cup chopped onion

1 small green bell pepper, chopped

1 celery rib, chopped

1 medium eggplant, peeled and chopped

¼ cup brown sugar

1½ teaspoons dried basil

¼ teaspoon garlic powder

¼ teaspoon salt

2 (8-ounce) cans no-salt-added tomato sauce

Nonstick cooking spray

1 cup water

1 cup low-fat shredded mozzarella cheese

1 slice bacon, cooked and crumbled

1. Add 2 teaspoons of olive oil to a medium saucepan on the stove and heat over medium-high heat.

2. Sauté the onion, bell pepper, celery, and eggplant for about 8 minutes.

3. Stir in the brown sugar, basil, garlic powder, salt, and tomato sauce.

4. Pour the water into the inner pot of the Instant Pot and place the trivet on top.

5. Generously spray a 7-inch round baking pan with nonstick cooking spray.

6. Place half of the eggplant mixture into the round baking pan. Sprinkle with half the cheese.

7. Repeat layers. Garnish with the crumbled bacon.

continued

Non-Pantry-Staple Grocery List
- 1 small green bell pepper
- 1 celery rib
- 1 medium eggplant
- 2 (8-ounce) cans no-salt-added tomato sauce
- 1 cup low-fat shredded mozzarella cheese
- 1 slice bacon

TIP
You may replace the olive oil with canola or grapeseed oil if you wish.

Calories 251
Fat 11 g
Fiber 5 g
Carbs 29 g
Net carbs 24 g
Sodium 1187 mg
Sugar 21 g
Protein 13 g

Main Dishes ✤ **83**

8. Place the 7-inch round baking pan on top of the trivet inside the inner pot.

9. Secure the lid and set the vent to sealing.

10. Manually set the cooking time for 10 minutes at high pressure.

11. When cooking time is up, manually release the pressure.

12. When the pin drops, remove the lid, then carefully remove the trivet with oven mitts. Allow the eggplant to cool for about 10 minutes before serving.

Serving Suggestion:
Simply serve alongside quinoa.

Eggplant Parmesan Lightened Up

Hope Comerford, Clinton Township, MI

Makes 4 servings
Prep. Time: 15 minutes ❧ Cooking Time: 10 minutes ❧ Setting: Manual
Pressure: High ❧ Release: Manual

1 large eggplant
Salt
1 cup water
Nonstick cooking spray
2 cups low-sodium, low-sugar marinara sauce, *divided*
½ teaspoon dried basil
¾ cup shredded Parmesan cheese

Serving Suggestion:
Serve this alongside your favorite healthy pasta.

Non-Pantry-Staple Grocery List
- 1 large eggplant
- 2 cups low-sodium, low-sugar marinara sauce
- ¾ cup shredded Parmesan cheese

Calories 159
Fat 9 g
Fiber 5 g
Carbs 16 g
Net carbs 9 g
Sodium 861 mg
Sugar 7 g
Protein 6 g

1. Prepare the eggplant by cutting the top and bottom off, then slicing it in long ¼-inch-thick slices. Lay the slices out on a baking sheet and sprinkle them with salt on both sides. Let them sit for a few minutes and then pat each side dry with a paper towel.

2. Pour the water into the inner pot of the Instant Pot and place the trivet on top.

3. Spray a 7-inch round baking pan with nonstick cooking spray.

4. Spread about ½ cup of marinara sauce on the bottom of the baking dish.

5. Begin layering your eggplant, a little marinara sauce, a sprinkle of basil, and a sprinkle of Parmesan until you have no more eggplant. End with sauce, a final sprinkle of basil, and Parmesan.

6. Secure the lid and set the vent to sealing.

7. Manually set the cook time to 10 minutes at high pressure.

8. When the cooking time is over, manually release the pressure.

9. When the pin drops, remove the lid and carefully remove the trivet with oven mitts. Allow the eggplant Parmesan to cool a bit before serving.

Moroccan Spiced Sweet Potato Medley

Pat Bishop, Bedminster, PA

Makes 6 main-dish servings
Prep. Time: 5 minutes & Cooking Time: 12 minutes & Setting: Sauté and Manual
Pressure: High & Release: Manual

2 teaspoons olive oil

1 medium onion, sliced

2 garlic cloves, crushed

$1\frac{1}{2}$ teaspoons ground coriander

$1\frac{1}{2}$ teaspoons ground cumin

$\frac{1}{4}$ teaspoon ground red pepper

2 medium (about $1\frac{1}{2}$ lb.) sweet potatoes, peeled and cut into $\frac{1}{2}$-inch-thick slices

14-ounce can no-salt-added stewed tomatoes

$\frac{3}{4}$ cup uncooked bulgur

$2\frac{1}{4}$ cups water

15-ounce can garbanzo beans, rinsed and drained

$\frac{1}{2}$ cup dark raisins

1 cup loosely packed fresh cilantro leaves, chopped

1. Set the Instant Pot to Sauté and heat up the olive oil in the inner pot.

2. Sauté the onion and garlic for 5 minutes.

3. Add the coriander, cumin, red pepper, sweet potatoes, tomatoes with their juices, bulgur, water, and garbanzo beans to the inner pot. Stir. Press Cancel.

4. Secure the lid and set the vent to sealing.

5. Manually set the cook time for 12 minutes on high pressure.

6. When the cooking time is over, manually release the pressure.

7. When the pin drops, remove the lid and stir in the raisins and cilantro.

8. Serve and enjoy!

Non-Pantry-Staple Grocery List
- $\frac{1}{4}$ teaspoon ground red pepper
- 2 medium sweet potatoes
- 14-ounce can no-salt-added stewed tomatoes
- $\frac{3}{4}$ cup bulgur
- 15-ounce can garbanzo beans
- $\frac{1}{2}$ cup dark raisins
- 1 cup fresh cilantro leaves

Calories 326
Fat 6 g
Fiber 11 g
Carbs 62 g
Net carbs 51 g
Sodium 340 mg
Sugar 15 g
Protein 11 g

TIP
You may replace the olive oil with coconut, canola, or grapeseed oil if you wish.

Garden Vegetable Crustless Quiche

Susan Kasting, Jenks, OK

Makes 4 servings
Prep. Time: 20 minutes ⚜ Cooking Time: 25 minutes ⚜ Setting: Manual
Pressure: High ⚜ Release: Natural then Manual ⚜ Standing Time: 10 minutes

1½ cups water
1½ cups egg substitute
3 large eggs
⅓ cup skim milk
½ cup whole wheat pastry flour
8 ounces low-sodium fat-free cottage cheese
Nonstick cooking spray
2 medium zucchini, sliced
½ small onion, diced
1 green bell pepper, finely chopped
½ lb. fresh mushrooms, sliced
½ cup chopped parsley
1 cup low-fat shredded cheese of your choice

Non-Pantry-Staple Grocery List
- ½ cup whole wheat pastry flour
- 8 ounces low-sodium fat-free cottage cheese
- 2 medium zucchini
- 1 green bell pepper
- ½ lb. sliced mushrooms
- ½ cup chopped parsley
- 1 cup low-fat shredded cheese of choice

Calories 289
Fat 7 g
Fiber 4 g
Carbs 25 g
Net carbs 21 g
Sodium 715 mg
Sugar 9 g
Protein 34 g

1. Pour the water into the inner pot of the Instant Pot and place the trivet on top.

2. In a large bowl, beat the egg substitute and eggs until fluffy.

3. Stir in the milk, flour, and cottage cheese.

4. In a pan coated with nonstick cooking spray, sauté the zucchini, onion, pepper, and mushrooms for 5 minutes.

5. Stir the sautéed vegetable mixture and parsley into the egg mixture.

6. When well combined, pour into a 7-inch round baking dish, lightly coated with cooking spray.

7. Top with cheese. Cover tightly with foil.

8. Place the baking pan on top of the trivet in the Instant Pot.

9. Secure the lid and set the vent to sealing.

10. Manually set the time for 25 minutes on high pressure.

11. When the cooking time is over, allow the pressure to release naturally for 10 minutes, then manually release the remaining pressure.

12. When the pin drops, remove the lid and carefully remove the trivet with oven mitts. Carefully remove the foil. Allow the quiche to stand 10 minutes before slicing.

Spinach Pie

Mary Ellen Musser, Reinholds, PA

Makes 4 main-dish servings
Prep. Time: 5 minutes & Cooking Time: 25 minutes & Setting: Manual
Pressure: High & Release: Natural then Manual & Standing Time: 10 minutes

2 cups low-sodium fat-free cottage cheese

10-ounce package frozen chopped spinach, thawed and squeezed dry

1 cup reduced-fat mozzarella cheese, shredded

Egg substitute equivalent to 4 eggs, or 8 egg whites, beaten

$\frac{1}{3}$ cup ($1\frac{1}{2}$ ounces) grated low-fat Parmesan cheese

1 teaspoon dried oregano

1 cup water

1. Mix all the ingredients in a large bowl.

2. Spoon into a lightly greased 7-inch round pan. Cover it tightly with foil.

3. Pour the water into the inner pot of the Instant Pot. Place the trivet on top.

4. Place the filled pan on top of the trivet.

5. Secure the lid and set the vent to sealing.

6. Manually set the cook time to 25 minutes on high pressure.

7. When the cooking time is over, let the pressure release naturally for 10 minutes, then manually release the remaining pressure.

8. When the pin drops, remove the lid and carefully lift the trivet and pan out with oven mitts. Remove the foil. Allow to stand for 10 minutes before cutting.

Non-Pantry-Staple Grocery List
- 1 cup reduced-fat mozzarella cheese
- 10-ounce package frozen spinach
- $\frac{1}{3}$ cup grated low-fat Parmesan cheese
- 2 cups low-sodium fat-free cottage cheese

Calories 304
Fat 12 g
Fiber 2 g
Carbs 14 g
Net carbs 63 g
Sodium 1036 mg
Sugar 6 g
Protein 35 g

Spinach Stuffed Tomatoes

Charlotte Hagner, Montague, MI

Makes 4 main-dish servings
Prep. Time: 15 minutes ⚜ Cooking Time: 1 minute ⚜ Setting: Manual
Pressure: High ⚜ Release: Manual

4 large, firm tomatoes

1 tablespoon olive oil

10-ounce package frozen spinach, thawed and squeezed dry

2 tablespoons finely chopped onion

½ cup fat-free half-and-half

2 egg whites, or egg substitute equivalent to 1 egg

1½ cups water

TIP
You may replace the olive oil with canola or grapeseed oil if you wish.

1. Slice off the top of each tomato. Remove the pulp and seeds.

2. Set the Instant Pot to the Sauté function and heat the olive oil in the inner pot.

3. Sauté the spinach and onion in the inner pot for about 5 minutes.

4. Hit Cancel on the Instant Pot.

5. In a small bowl, combine the half-and-half and egg whites or egg substitute.

6. Stir in the sautéed spinach and onion. Spoon this mixture into the tomatoes.

7. Add the water to the inner pot and place the trivet on top.

8. Arrange the filled tomatoes on top of the trivet inside the inner pot.

9. Secure the lid and set the vent to sealing.

Non-Pantry-Staple Grocery List
- 4 large, firm tomatoes
- 10-ounce package frozen spinach
- ½ cup fat-free half-and-half

Calories 110

Fat 5 g

Fiber 4 g

Carbs 11 g

Net carbs 7 g

Sodium 117 mg

Sugar 6 g

Protein 6 g

10. Manually set the cook time for 1 minute on high pressure.

11. When the cooking time is over, manually release the pressure.

12. When the pin drops, remove the lid and very carefully remove the trivet from the inner pot with oven mitts.

13. Carefully place the stuffed tomatoes on a serving platter. Serve warm and enjoy!

Serving Suggestion:
Serve with Perfect Sweet Potatoes from page 145.

Summer Squash Pie

Natalia Showalter, Mt. Solon, VA

Makes 4 main-dish servings
Prep. Time: 20 minutes ❧ Cooking Time: 25 minutes ❧ Setting: Manual
Pressure: High ❧ Release: Manual ❧ Standing Time: 10 minutes

3 cups shredded summer squash

2 tablespoons olive oil

½ cup chopped onion

½ cup shredded carrot

2 teaspoons olive oil

2 egg whites, or egg substitute equivalent to 1 egg

½ cup fat-free sour cream

¾ cup shredded low-sodium, low-fat mozzarella cheese

2 tablespoons fresh minced parsley

¼ teaspoon pepper

¼ teaspoon dried oregano

¼ teaspoon garlic powder

½ cup cracker crumbs, from about 5 whole crackers with unsalted tops, crushed

1½ cups water

Non-Pantry-Staple Grocery List
- 2 summer squash
- 1½ carrots
- ½ cup fat-free sour cream
- ¾ cup low-sodium, low-fat shredded mozzarella cheese
- 2 tablespoons fresh minced parsley
- 5 crackers

1. Place the shredded squash into a clean cloth kitchen towel. Fold the towel over the squash and twist or press the towel to remove moisture.

2. Set the Instant Pot to Sauté and heat the oil in the inner pot.

3. Sauté the squash, onion, and carrot in the heated olive oil for about 8 minutes. Hit Cancel.

4. In a bowl, mix the egg whites or egg substitute, sour cream, cheese, parsley, and seasonings. Stir in the sautéed vegetables.

5. Pour into 7-inch round pan or baking dish.

6. Garnish the top with cracker crumbs.

7. Wipe out the inner pot with a paper towel.

8. Pour the water into the inner pot. Place the trivet on top.

TIP
You may replace the olive oil with coconut, canola, or grapeseed oil if you wish.

Calories 345
Fat 22 g
Fiber 2 g
Carbs 23 g
Net carbs 21 g
Sodium 482 mg
Sugar 4.5 g
Protein 15 g

9. Place the filled round pan/baking dish on top of the trivet.

10. Secure the lid and set the vent to sealing.

11. Manually set the cook time to 25 minutes.

12. When the cooking time is over, manually release the pressure.

13. When the pin drops, remove the lid. Carefully remove the trivet and pan/dish with oven mitts. Allow to stand 10 minutes before cutting.

Mushroom Risotto

Hope Comerford, Clinton Township, MI

Makes 4 servings
Prep. Time: 7 minutes ⚘ Cooking Time: 6 minutes ⚘ Setting: Manual
Pressure: High ⚘ Release: Manual

1 tablespoon extra-virgin olive oil

½ cup finely chopped onion

2 garlic cloves, minced

½ cup chopped baby bella mushrooms

½ cup chopped shiitake mushrooms

¼ teaspoon salt

⅛ teaspoon pepper

1 cup uncooked arborio rice

2 cups low sodium chicken stock

½ cup frozen peas, thawed

¼ cup freshly grated low-fat Parmesan cheese

1 tablespoon butter or margarine, *optional*

1. Set the Instant Pot to the Sauté function and heat the oil in the inner pot.

2. Sauté the onion and garlic for 3 minutes. Add the mushrooms, salt, and pepper, and continue sautéing for an additional 3 to 4 minutes.

3. Press Cancel. Stir in the rice and chicken stock. Secure the lid and set the vent to sealing.

4. Manually set the cook time for 6 minutes on high pressure.

5. When the cooking time is over, manually release the pressure.

6. When the pin drops, remove the lid and stir in the peas, grated Parmesan, and butter or margarine (if using). Let the peas heat through for about 2 minutes, then serve.

TIP
You may replace the olive oil with canola or grapeseed oil if you wish.

Non-Pantry-Staple Grocery List
- ½ cup chopped baby bella mushrooms
- ½ cup chopped shiitake mushrooms
- 1 cup arborio rice
- ½ cup frozen peas
- ¼ cup freshly grated low-fat Parmesan cheese

Calories 186

Fat 6 g

Fiber 3 g

Carbs 26 g

Net carbs 23 g

Sodium 385 mg

Sugar 4 g

Protein 8 g

Main Dishes 95

Pumpkin Risotto

Marilyn Mowry, Irving, TX

Makes 4 servings
Prep. Time: 3 minutes ❧ Cooking Time: 6 minutes ❧ Setting: Manual
Pressure: High ❧ Release: Manual

1 tablespoon olive oil

2 onions, chopped

1 garlic clove, minced

1 cup raw arborio rice

1 cup dry white wine

1 cup low-sodium chicken stock

1 cup canned pumpkin puree

$1/4$ cup grated low-fat Parmesan cheese

Pepper to taste

$1/8$ teaspoon ground nutmeg

1. Set the Instant Pot to the Sauté function and heat the oil in the inner pot.

2. Sauté the onions and garlic for 3 minutes.

3. Press Cancel. Stir in the rice, wine, and chicken stock. Secure the lid and set the vent to sealing.

4. Manually set the cook time for 6 minutes on high pressure.

5. When the cooking time is over, manually release the pressure.

6. When the pin drops, remove the lid and stir in the pumpkin, cheese, and pepper. Let it heat through for a few minutes. Sprinkle with the nutmeg. Serve at once.

TIP
You may replace the olive oil with canola or grapeseed oil if you wish.

Non-Pantry-Staple Grocery List
- 1 cup arborio rice
- 1 cup dry white wine
- 1 cup canned pumpkin puree
- $1/4$ cup grated low-fat Parmesan cheese
- $1/8$ teaspoon ground nutmeg

Calories 196

Fat 5 g

Fiber 2 g

Carbs 23 g

Net carbs 21 g

Sodium 169 mg

Sugar 4 g

Protein 4.5 g

Barley Risotto with Grilled Peppers

Jean Turner, Williams Lake, BC

Makes 4 servings
Prep. Time: 23 minutes ❧ Cooking Time: 20 minutes ❧ Setting: Manual
Pressure: High ❧ Release: Natural then Manual

1 red bell pepper

1 yellow bell pepper

1 tablespoon olive oil

1 cup chopped onions

2 teaspoons garlic, minced

3 cups low-sodium chicken stock, *divided*

1 cup raw pearl barley

3 tablespoons grated low-fat Parmesan cheese

¼ teaspoon ground black pepper

TIP
You may replace the olive oil with canola or grapeseed oil if you wish.

1. Cut the red and yellow bell peppers in half and remove the seeds. Place on a baking sheet, cut-side down. Cook under preheated broiler, turning occasionally, for 20 minutes, or until charred on all sides.

2. Remove from the oven. When the peppers are cool enough to handle, peel, stem, and core them. Cut into chunks. Set aside.

3. Set the Instant Pot to the Sauté function and heat the oil in the inner pot.

4. Sauté the onion and garlic for 3 minutes. Press Cancel.

5. Stir in the stock, barley, and grilled peppers. Secure the lid and set the vent to sealing.

6. Manually set the cook time for 20 minutes on high pressure.

7. When the cooking time is over, let the pressure release naturally for 5 minutes, then manually release the remaining pressure.

8. When the pin drops, remove the lid and stir in Parmesan cheese and pepper. Serve immediately.

Non-Pantry-Staple Grocery List
- 1 red bell pepper
- 1 yellow bell pepper
- 1 cup pearl barley
- 3 tablespoons grated low-fat Parmesan cheese

Calories 300

Fat 8 g

Fiber 9 g

Carbs 45 g

Net carbs 36 g

Sodium 380 mg

Sugar 6 g

Protein 12 g

Quinoa with Spinach

Karen Ceneviva, New Haven, CT

Makes 4 servings
Prep. Time: 2 minutes & Cooking Time: 1 minute & Setting: Manual
Pressure: High & Release: Natural

1½ cups raw quinoa

2¼ cups water

3 tablespoons freshly squeezed lemon juice

2 tablespoons extra-virgin olive oil

¼ teaspoon sea salt

Pepper to taste, *optional*

2 cups fresh spinach leaves, well washed, dried, and chopped

3 large scallions, thinly sliced

3 tablespoons fresh dill

1. Rinse and drain the quinoa.

2. Pour the quinoa and water into the inner pot of the Instant Pot. Secure the lid and set the vent to sealing.

3. Manually set the time for 1 minute on high pressure.

4. When the cooking time is over, let the pressure release naturally.

5. When the pin drops, remove the lid. Stir in the lemon juice, olive oil, sea salt, and pepper (if using).

6. Stir in the spinach, scallions, and dill.

7. Serve warm, or at room temperature.

TIP
You may replace the olive oil with canola or grapeseed oil if you wish.

Non-Pantry-Staple Grocery List
- 1½ cups quinoa
- 3 tablespoons freshly squeezed lemon juice
- 2 cups fresh spinach leaves
- 3 large scallions
- 3 tablespoons fresh dill

Calories 339
Fat 11 g
Fiber 7 g
Carbs 52 g
Net carbs 45 g
Sodium 118 mg
Sugar 9 g
Protein 10 g

Pasta Primavera

Hope Comerford, Clinton Township, MI

Makes 6 servings
Prep. Time: 10 minutes   ⚜   Cooking Time: 5 minutes (may vary due to pasta chosen)
Setting: Sauté and Manual   ⚜   Pressure: High   ⚜   Release: Manual

2 cups chopped broccolini tops

½ lb. baby bella mushrooms, sliced

2 small zucchini, sliced into ¼-inch-thick rounds

1 cup sliced cherry tomatoes

3 garlic cloves, sliced

½ teaspoon salt

⅛ teaspoon pepper

2 tablespoons olive oil, *divided*

8 ounces pasta of your choice

4 cups reduced-sodium vegetable stock

¼ cup grated reduced-fat Parmesan cheese

2 tablespoons chopped fresh basil

Non-Pantry-Staple Grocery List
- 2 cups chopped broccolini tops
- ½ lb. baby bella mushrooms
- 2 small zucchini
- 1 cup sliced cherry tomatoes
- 8 ounces pasta of your choice
- ¼ cup grated reduced-fat Parmesan cheese
- 2 tablespoons chopped fresh basil

TIP
You may replace the olive oil with canola or grapeseed oil if you wish.

Calories 282
Fat 8 g
Fiber 4 g
Carbs 41 g
Net carbs 37 g
Sodium 458 mg
Sugar 6 g
Protein 12 g

1. In a large bowl, toss the broccolini, mushrooms, zucchini, cherry tomatoes, garlic, salt, and pepper with 1 tablespoon olive oil.

2. Set the Instant Pot to Sauté and heat the additional tablespoon of olive oil.

3. Pour the vegetables into the inner pot. Stir regularly for about 7 minutes, or until the vegetables are tender. Put them back in the large bowl you had them in and cover to keep them warm.

4. Press Cancel on the Instant Pot. Pour the pasta and vegetable stock into the inner pot and secure the lid. Set the vent to sealing.

5. Manually set the cook time for 5 minutes on high pressure, or half of whatever time the package instructions say to cook your pasta of choice for.

6. When the cooking time is over, manually release the pressure.

7. When the pin drops, remove the lid. Use a ladle to remove 1 cup of the cooking liquid. Pour this into the bowl with vegetables.

8. Wearing oven mitts, carefully remove the inner pot and drain the pasta into a colander.

9. Pour the drained pasta into the large bowl with the reserved cooking liquid and vegetables. Add the Parmesan cheese and fresh basil. Toss and enjoy!

Lentils with Cheese

Kay Nussbaum, Salem, OR
Laura R. Showalter, Dayton, VA
Natalia Showalter, Mt. Solon, VA

Makes 6 servings
Prep. Time: 2 minutes & Cooking Time: 10 minutes & Setting: Manual
Pressure: High & Release: Manual

1½ cups raw lentils, rinsed

3 cups water

½ teaspoon salt

¼ teaspoon pepper

⅛ teaspoon dried marjoram

⅛ teaspoon dried sage

⅛ teaspoon dried thyme

2 large onions, chopped

2 garlic cloves, minced

14.5-ounce can low-sodium diced tomatoes

2 large carrots, sliced ⅛-inch thick

½ cup thinly sliced celery

1 bell pepper, chopped, *optional*

1 cup (4 ounces) low-fat, low-sodium shredded cheddar cheese

1. Place the lentils, water, salt, pepper, marjoram, sage, thyme, onions, garlic, tomatoes, carrots, celery, and bell pepper into the inner pot of the Instant Pot.

2. Secure the lid and set the vent to sealing.

3. Manually set the cook time for 10 minutes on high pressure.

4. When the cooking time is over, manually release the pressure.

5. When the pin drops, remove the lid. Stir in the shredded cheddar cheese.

Non-Pantry-Staple Grocery List
- 1½ cups lentils
- ⅛ teaspoon marjoram
- ⅛ teaspoon dried sage
- 14.5-ounce can low-sodium diced tomatoes
- 2 large carrots
- ½ cup thinly sliced celery
- 1 cup low-fat, low-sodium shredded cheddar cheese
- 1 bell pepper, *optional*

Calories 98

Fat 2 g

Fiber 2 g

Carbs 13 g

Net carbs 11 g

Sodium 496 mg

Sugar 4 g

Protein 8 gv

Barbacoa Beef

Cindy Herren, West Des Moines, IA

Makes 6–8 servings
Prep. Time: 20 minutes ♣ Cooking Time: 60 minutes ♣ Setting: Sauté then Manual
Pressure: High ♣ Release: Manual

5 garlic cloves

½ medium onion

Juice of 1 lime

2–4 tablespoons chipotles in adobo sauce (to taste)

1 teaspoon ground cumin

1 teaspoon ground oregano

½ teaspoon ground cloves

1 cup water

3 lb. beef eye of round or bottom round roast, all fat trimmed

2½ teaspoon kosher salt

Black pepper

1 teaspoon oil

3 bay leaves

½ teaspoon salt, *optional*

½ teaspoon cumin, *optional*

1. Place the garlic, onion, lime juice, chipotles, cumin, oregano, cloves, and water in a blender and puree until smooth.

2. Trim all the fat off the meat and then cut the meat into 3-inch pieces. Season with the salt and black pepper.

3. Set the Instant Pot to Sauté. When hot, add the oil and brown the meat, in batches on all sides, about 5 minutes.

4. Press Cancel. Add all of the browned meat, sauce from the blender, and bay leaves to the inner pot.

5. Secure the lid and set the vent to sealing.

6. Cook on high pressure for 60 minutes.

7. Manually release the pressure once cook time is up.

8. Remove the meat and place in a dish. Shred with two forks, and reserve 1½ cups of the liquid. Discard the bay leaves and the remaining liquid.

9. Return the shredded meat to the pot, add ½ teaspoon salt (or to taste), ½ tsp cumin, and the 1½ cups of the reserved liquid.

Serving Suggestion:
Serve with fresh salsa, sour cream, and corn over Cilantro Lime Rice (see recipe on page 156).

Non-Pantry-Staple Grocery List
- 1 lime
- 2–4 chipotles in adobo sauce
- ½ teaspoon ground cloves
- 3 lb. beef eye of round or bottom round roast

Calories 450
Fat 33 g
Fiber 0.5 g
Carbs 3 g
Net carbs 2.5 g
Sodium 760 mg
Sugar 1 g
Protein 33 g

Braised Beef with Cranberries

Audrey L. Kneer, Williamsfield, IL

Makes 8 servings

Prep. Time: 20 minutes ♣ Cooking Time: 60 minutes ♣ Pressure: High ♣ Release: Natural then Manual

2 lb. sliced, well-trimmed top round beef

$\frac{1}{8}$ teaspoon pepper

1 tablespoon olive oil

$\frac{1}{2}$ cup peeled and diced turnip

1 medium onion, chopped

2 garlic cloves, chopped

1 medium carrot, chopped

1 celery rib, cut fine

1 cup low-sugar apple juice

1 cup fresh or frozen cranberries

1 sprig parsley

1 bay leaf

Non-Pantry-Staple Grocery List
- 2 lb. top round beef
- $\frac{1}{2}$ cup diced turnip
- 1 medium carrot
- 1 celery rib
- 1 cup low-sugar apple juice
- 1 cup fresh or frozen cranberries
- 1 sprig parsley

Calories 235
Fat 6 g
Fiber 1 g
Carbs 9 g
Net carbs 8 g
Sodium 98 mg
Sugar 5 g
Protein 34 g

TIP
You may replace the olive oil with canola or grapeseed oil if you wish.

1. Rub the beef with the pepper. Set aside.

2. Set the Instant Pot to Sauté and heat the olive oil in the inner pot.

3. Sauté the beef for about 10 minutes, searing each side.

4. Remove the beef and set it aside.

5. Sauté the onion and garlic for about 3 minutes, then add the carrot and celery and continue sautéing for about 5 more minutes.

6. Pour in the apple juice and scrape the bottom of the pot to "deglaze."

7. Press Cancel. Add the beef back in, and add the cranberries, parsley, and bay leaf. Make sure the sprig of parsley and bay leaf are tucked into the liquid.

8. Secure the lid and set the vent to sealing.

9. Set the cook time manually for 60 minutes on high pressure.

10. When the cooking time is over, let the pressure release naturally for 10 minutes, then manually release the remaining pressure.

Serving Suggestion:
Serve alongside Orange-Glazed Parsnips from page 152.

Mexican-Inspired Bottom Round Roast

David Ecker, Fair Lawn, NJ

Makes 4–6 servings

Prep. Time: 5 minutes ❧ Cooking Time: 6 hours ❧ Setting: Slow Cooker Medium or Normal

½ teaspoon crushed red pepper flakes (adjust to taste)

½ teaspoon chipotle pepper flakes (adjust to taste)

1 teaspoon cumin

1 teaspoon chili powder

1 teaspoon kosher salt

2½–3 lb. bottom round roast

15-ounce container of Whole Foods Taqueria Salsa or Medium Salsa

1. Mix the spices, then rub the roast with them.

2. Place the seasoned bottom round roast in the inner pot of the Instant Pot.

3. Pour the salsa on top roast.

4. Cover the Instant Pot with the fitting glass lid. Press Slow Cook Normal setting and adjust time to 6 hours.

Serving Suggestion:

Shred the meat and serve with 12 to 16 ounces of tagliatelle pasta cooked separately al dente and then tossed with the meat in a bowl (this will provide 8 to 10 servings).

Non-Pantry-Staple Grocery List
- ½ teaspoon crushed red pepper flakes
- ½ teaspoon chipotle pepper flakes
- 2½–3 lb. bottom round roast.
- 15-ounce container of Whole Foods Taqueria Salsa or Medium Salsa

---

Calories 317

Fat 11 g

Fiber 1.5 g

Carbs 5 g

Net carbs 3.5 g

Sodium 997 mg

Sugar 3 g

Protein 50 g

Beef and Zucchini Casserole

Judi Manos, West Islip, NY

Makes 6 servings

Prep. Time: 12 minutes ♣ Cooking Time: 22 minutes ♣ Setting: Sauté and Manual
Pressure: High ♣ Release: Natural

2 teaspoons canola oil

$\frac{1}{2}$ cup finely chopped onion

1 lb. 95% lean ground beef

1 lb. (3 small) zucchini, cut into $\frac{1}{4}$-inch-thick slices

$\frac{1}{4}$ lb. fresh mushrooms, sliced

14.5-ounce can no-salt-added diced tomatoes

$\frac{1}{2}$ teaspoon garlic powder

$\frac{1}{2}$ teaspoon dried oregano

1 cup brown rice

2 cup water

$\frac{1}{4}$ cup grated low-fat Parmesan cheese

TIP
You may replace the canola oil with olive or grapeseed oil if you wish.

1. Set the Instant Pot to Sauté and heat the oil in the inner pot.

2. Sauté the onion for about 3 minutes, then add the ground beef and sauté for about 8 more minutes, or until the beef is no longer pink.

3. Press Cancel. Add the remaining ingredients, except for the grated Parmesan cheese, into the inner pot in the order shown.

4. Secure the lid and set the vent to sealing.

5. Manually set the cook time for 22 minutes on high pressure.

6. When the cooking time is over, let the pressure release naturally.

7. When the pin drops, remove the lid and stir in the Parmesan cheese. Serve and enjoy!

Non-Pantry-Staple Grocery List
- 1 lb. 95% lean ground beef
- 3 small zucchini
- $\frac{1}{4}$ lb. mushrooms, sliced
- 14.5-ounce can no-salt-added diced tomatoes
- $\frac{1}{4}$ cup grated low-fat Parmesan cheese

Calories 287
Fat 7 g
Fiber 3 g
Carbs 37 g
Net carbs 34 g
Sodium 226 mg
Sugar 4 g
Protein 22 g

Stuffed Cabbage

Hope Comerford, Clinton Township, MI

Makes 12–15 stuffed cabbage rolls
Prep. Time: 30 minutes ❧ Cooking Time: 20 minutes ❧ Setting: Sauté and Manual
Pressure: High ❧ Release: Natural and Manual

12 cups water

1 large head cabbage (you will use about 12–15 leaves)

1 lb. 95% lean ground beef

1 medium onion, chopped

2 garlic cloves, chopped

1 teaspoon chopped fresh parsley

¼ teaspoon salt

½ teaspoon pepper

1 egg, beaten

¾ cup brown rice, uncooked

1 cup water

1 tablespoon vinegar

16 ounces low-sugar, low-sodium marinara sauce, *divided*

2 teaspoons Italian seasoning

1. Pour the water into the inner pot and press Sauté on the Instant pot. Bring the water to a boil.

2. Gently lower the cabbage into the water and cook for about 5 minutes, turning to be sure all the outer leaves are softened. Press Cancel.

3. Remove the cabbage and carefully drain the water. Peel off 12 to 15 leaves.

4. In a bowl, mix the ground beef, onion, garlic, parsley, salt, pepper, egg, and brown rice with a wooden spoon or clean hands.

5. On a clean surface, lay out the cabbage leaves. (You made need to thin some of the thicker ribs of the cabbage leaves with a paring knife.) Evenly divide the filling between the leaves. Roll them burrito style, tucking in the ends and rolling tightly. If you need to, you can use a toothpick to hold them closed.

Non-Pantry-Staple Grocery List
- 1 large head cabbage
- 1 lb. 95% fat-free ground beef
- 1 teaspoon fresh chopped parsley
- 1 tablespoon vinegar
- 16 ounces low-sugar, low-sodium marinara sauce
- 2 teaspoons Italian seasoning

Calories 305

Fat 10 g

Fiber 5 g

Carbs 31 g

Net carbs 26 g

Sodium 752 mg

Sugar 7 g

Protein 24 g

6. Pour the water and vinegar into the inner pot. Gently place the cabbage rolls into the pot, pouring a little sauce on top of each layer and finishing with a layer of sauce. Sprinkle with the Italian seasoning.

7. Secure the lid and set the vent to sealing.

8. Set the Instant Pot to cook manually for 20 minutes on high pressure.

9. When the cooking time is over, let the pressure release naturally for 20 minutes and then manually release the remaining pressure.

10. When the pin drops, remove the lid. Serve hot.

Ginger Pork Chops

Mary Fisher, Leola, PA

Makes 4 servings
Prep. Time: 10 minutes ⚘ *Cooking Time: 1 minute* ⚘ *Setting: Sauté and Manual*
Pressure: High ⚘ *Release: Natural then Manual*

$\frac{1}{3}$ cup low-sodium soy sauce or tamari

$\frac{1}{3}$ cup honey

2 garlic cloves, minced

Dash ground ginger

1 tablespoon olive oil

4–5 thick-cut boneless pork chops (1 inch to 1$\frac{1}{2}$ inches thick)

$\frac{1}{8}$ teaspoon pepper

1 tablespoon cornstarch

1 tablespoon cold water

2 tablespoons sliced scallions

TIP
You may replace the olive oil with canola or grapeseed oil if you wish.

Non-Pantry-Staple Grocery List
- 4–5 thick-cut boneless pork chops
- $\frac{1}{3}$ cup low-sodium soy sauce or tamari
- Dash ground ginger
- 2 tablespoons sliced scallions

1. In a bowl, mix the soy sauce, honey, and ginger. Set aside

2. Set the Instant Pot to Sauté and heat the olive oil in the inner pot.

3. Season the pork chops on each side with a bit of pepper and then sear them in the inner pot. Only cook them for 1 to 2 minutes per side. Remove them and set them aside.

4. Add the garlic to the inner pot and sauté for about 2 minutes. Add the sauce you made in the bowl earlier and stir, scraping the bottom of the pot with a wooden spoon.

5. Press Cancel. Place the pork chops into the sauce, including any juices the pork chops released while resting.

6. Secure the lid and set the vent to sealing. Set the Instant Pot to manually cook for 1 minute on high pressure.

continued

Calories 301
Fat 10 g
Fiber 0.5 g
Carbs 27 g
Net carbs 26.5 g
Sodium 1390 mg
Sugar 23 g
Protein 26 g

7. When the cooking time is over, let the pressure release naturally for 5 minutes, then release the rest of the pressure manually.

8. When the pin drops, remove the lid and remove the pork chops. Set them aside on a clean plate or serving platter.

9. Mix the cornstarch and cold water. Set the Instant Pot to Sauté once more and whisk in this mixture into the sauce in the inner pot. Let the sauce thicken to your liking, stirring often.

10. When you are ready to serve, pour some of the sauce over each pork chop and sprinkle with scallion.

Serving Suggestion:
Serve with Squash Apple Bake from page 143.

Paprika Pork Chops with Rice

Sharon Easter, Yuba City, CA

Makes 4 servings
Prep. Time: 5 minutes   Cooking Time: 30 minutes   Setting: Sauté and Manual
Pressure: High   Release: Manual

⅛ teaspoon pepper

1 teaspoon paprika

1 tablespoon olive oil

4–5 thick-cut boneless pork chops (1 inch to 1½ inches thick)

1¼ cups water, *divided*

1 onion, sliced

½ green bell pepper, sliced in rings

1½ cups canned no-salt-added stewed tomatoes

1 cup brown rice

TIP
You may replace the olive oil with canola or grapeseed oil if you wish.

Non-Pantry-Staple Grocery List
- 4–5 thick-cut boneless pork chops
- ½ green bell pepper
- 1½ cups canned no-salt-added stewed tomatoes

1. Mix the pepper and paprika in a flat dish. Dredge the chops in the seasoning mixture.

2. Set the Instant Pot to the Sauté function and heat the oil in the inner pot.

3. Brown the chops on both sides for 1 to 2 minutes a side. Remove the pork chops and set aside.

4. Pour a small amount of water into the inner pot and scrape up any bits from the bottom with a wooden spoon. Press Cancel.

5. Place the browned chops side by side in the inner pot. Place 1 slice onion and 1 ring of green pepper on top of each chop. Spoon tomatoes with their juices over the top.

6. Pour the rice in and pour the remaining water over the top.

7. Secure the lid and set the vent to sealing.

8. Manually set the cook time for 30 minutes on high pressure.

9. When the cooking time is over, manually release the pressure.

Calories 427
Fat 14 g
Fiber 3 g
Carbs 40 g
Net carbs 37 g
Sodium 127 mg
Sugar 2 g
Protein 35 g

Healthy Joes

Gladys M. High, Ephrata, PA

Makes 4–5 servings
Prep. Time: 15 minutes ☙ Cooking Time: 10 minutes ☙ Setting: Sauté and Manual
Pressure: High ☙ Release: Natural then Manual

1 tablespoon olive oil

1 cup chopped onion

2 garlic cloves, chopped

1 medium bell pepper, chopped

1 medium zucchini, shredded, *optional*

1 lb. 90% lean ground pork loin

1½ cups no-salt-added diced tomatoes

1 tablespoon chili powder

1 teaspoon paprika

Black pepper to taste

½ cup water

¾ cup no-salt-added tomato sauce

1 tablespoon no-salt-added tomato paste

1½ tablespoon brown sugar

4–5 whole wheat hamburger buns

1. Set the Instant Pot to Sauté and heat the oil in the inner pot.

2. Sauté the onion and garlic for about 3 minutes. Add the bell pepper and zucchini (if using) and continue to sauté for about 5 minutes.

3. Add the ground pork to the inner pot and continue to cook for about 4 minutes. Press Cancel.

4. Pour in the tomatoes, chili powder, paprika, black pepper, water, tomato sauce, tomato paste, and brown sugar. Stir to combine all ingredients.

5. Secure the lid and set the vent to sealing.

6. Manually set the cook time for 10 minutes at high pressure.

7. When the cooking time is over, let the pressure release naturally for 5 minutes, then manually release the remaining pressure.

8. When the pin drops, remove the lid, stir. Spoon the mixture into the buns and enjoy.

Non-Pantry-Staple Grocery List
- 1 medium bell pepper
- 1 medium zucchini, *optional*
- 1 lb. 90% lean ground pork loin
- 1½ cups no-salt-added diced tomatoes
- ¾ cup no-salt-added tomato sauce
- 1 tablespoon no-salt-added tomato paste
- 4–5 whole wheat hamburger buns

Calories 503

Fat 23 g

Fiber 8 g

Carbs 46 g

Net carbs 38 g

Sodium 777 mg

Sugar 12 g

Protein 30 g

TIP

You may replace the olive oil with canola or grapeseed oil if you wish.

Chicken Dinner in a Packet

Bonnie Whaling, Clearfield, PA

Makes 4 servings
Prep. Time: 10 minutes ❧ Cooking Time: 15 minutes ❧ Setting: Manual
Pressure: High ❧ Release: Natural

1 cup water

4 (5-ounce) boneless, skinless chicken breast halves

2 cups sliced fresh mushrooms

2 medium carrots, cut in thin strips, about 1 cup

1 medium zucchini, unpeeled and sliced, about 1½ cups

2 tablespoons olive oil or canola oil

2 tablespoons lemon juice

1 tablespoon fresh basil or 1 teaspoon dry basil

¼ teaspoon salt

¼ teaspoon black pepper

Non-Pantry-Staple Grocery List
- 4 (5 ounce) boneless, skinless chicken breast halves
- 2 cups sliced mushrooms
- 2 medium carrots
- 1 medium zucchini
- 2 tablespoons lemon juice
- 1 tablespoon fresh basil (or use dry)

Calories 275
Fat 11 g
Fiber 3 g
Carbs 35 g
Net carbs 32 g
Sodium 218 mg
Sugar 4 g
Protein 35 g

TIP
You may replace the olive oil with canola or grapeseed oil if you wish.

1. Pour the water into the inner pot of the Instant Pot and place the trivet or a steamer basket on top.

2. Fold four 12-inch × 28-inch pieces of foil in half to make four 12-inch × 14-inch rectangles. Place one chicken breast half on each piece of foil.

3. Top with the mushrooms, carrots, and zucchini, dividing the vegetables equally between the chicken bundles.

4. In a small bowl, stir together the oil, lemon juice, basil, salt, and pepper.

5. Drizzle the oil mixture over the vegetables and chicken.

6. Pull up two opposite edges of foil. Seal with a double fold. Then fold in the remaining edges, leaving enough space for steam to build.

7. Place the bundles on top of the trivet, or inside the steamer basket.

8. Secure the lid and set the vent to sealing.

9. Manually set the cook time for 15 minutes at high pressure.

10. When the cooking time is over, let the pressure release naturally. When the pin drops, remove the lid.

11. Serve dinners in foil packets, or transfer to serving plate.

Skinny Chicken Stroganoff

Carol Sherwood, Batavia, NY

Makes 6 servings
Prep. Time: 10 minutes ⚭ Cooking Time: 5 minutes ⚭ Setting: Sauté and Manual
Pressure: High ⚭ Release: Natural then Manual

1 teaspoon olive oil

1 cup chopped onion

1 garlic clove, pressed

1½ lb. boneless, skinless chicken breasts, cut into bite-size pieces

⅛ teaspoon black pepper

8 ounces uncooked whole wheat wide egg noodles

8 ounces sliced fresh mushrooms

1 cup low-fat low-sodium chicken broth

¾ cup reduced-fat sour cream

4 slices turkey bacon, cooked and broken, *optional*

2 tablespoons chopped fresh parsley, *optional*

2 tablespoons cornstarch

2 tablespoons cold water

1. Set the Instant Pot to Sauté and heat the olive oil in the inner pot.

2. Sauté the onion and garlic for 3 minutes. Press Cancel.

3. Add the chicken and pepper. Stir to coat everything in the pot. Pour the noodles on top of the chicken mixture. Evenly spread out. Evenly spread the mushrooms on top of the noodles.

4. Pour the chicken broth on top. Secure the lid and set the vent to sealing.

5. Manually set the cook time for 2 minutes at high pressure.

6. When the cooking time is over, let the pressure release naturally for 10 minutes, then manually release the remaining pressure.

7. When the pin drops, remove the lid. Stir.

8. Remove about ¼ cup of the liquid from the inner pot, and, in a separate bowl, mix this with the sour cream, tempering it. Slowly add this tempered sour cream to the inner pot, stirring constantly. Stir in the bacon and parsley if desired.

9. Set the Instant Pot to Sauté. In a small bowl, whisk together the cornstarch and water. Add this to the inner pot and stir. Cook for a couple of minutes, or until thickened to your liking, then press Cancel.

Non-Pantry-Staple Grocery List
- 1½ lb. boneless, skinless chicken breasts
- 8 ounces sliced mushrooms
- 8 ounces whole wheat wide egg noodles
- ¾ cup reduced-fat sour cream
- 4 slices turkey bacon, *optional*
- 2 tablespoons chopped fresh parsley, *optional*

Calories 483

Fat 15 g

Fiber 2 g

Carbs 37 g

Net carbs 35 g

Sodium 268 mg

Sugar 3 g

Protein 49 g

TIP
You may replace the olive oil with canola or grapeseed oil if you wish.

Chicken Rice Bake

Nanci Keatley, Salem, OR

Makes 6 servings
Prep. Time: 8 minutes ❦ Cooking Time: 22 minutes ❦ Setting: Sauté and Manual
Pressure: High ❦ Release: Manual ❦ Standing Time: 10 minutes

1 tablespoon olive oil

1 cup finely diced onions

1 teaspoon garlic, chopped

1 cup chopped celery

2 lb. boneless, skinless chicken breasts, cut into bite-size pieces

1 cup chopped carrots

2 cups sliced fresh mushrooms

1½ cups uncooked brown rice

1½ teaspoons salt

1 teaspoon pepper

1 teaspoon dill weed

1½ cups low-sodium chicken broth

1. Set the Instant Pot to the Sauté function and heat the oil in the inner pot.

2. Sauté the onions and garlic for 3 minutes. Add the celery and sauté an additional 3 minutes.

3. Press Cancel. Add the chicken and spread out evenly, Add the carrots and mushrooms and spread out evenly.

4. Pour the rice evenly on top and sprinkle with the seasonings. Last, pour in the chicken broth. Do not stir.

5. Set the cook time manually to cook for 22 minutes on high pressure.

6. When the cooking time is over, manually release the pressure.

7. Allow to stand 10 minutes before serving.

TIP
You may replace the olive oil with canola or grapeseed oil if you wish.

Non-Pantry-Staple Grocery List
- 1 cup chopped celery
- 2 lb. boneless, skinless chicken breasts
- 1 cup chopped carrots
- 2 cups sliced mushrooms
- 1 teaspoon dill weed

Calories 523
Fat 12 g
Fiber 3 g
Carbs 44 g
Net carbs 41 g
Sodium 715 mg
Sugar 4 g
Protein 57 g

Cheesy Chicken and Rice

Amanda Breeden, Timberville, VA

Makes 5–6 servings
Prep. Time: 5 minutes ⚘ Cooking Time: 30 minutes ⚘ Setting: Manual
Pressure: High ⚘ Release: Manual

3 cups low-sodium chicken broth

2 cups brown rice

1 lb. frozen boneless, skinless chicken breasts

3 cups shredded reduced-fat cheddar cheese

TIP
Some like more or less cheese. Add more if desired.

1. Add the chicken broth, rice, and frozen chicken to the inner pot of the Instant Pot.

2. Secure the lid and set the vent to sealing. Cook on high pressure setting for 30 minutes.

3. When done cooking, release the pressure manually and stir everything together.

4. Stir the cheese into the dish until it is melted and blended evenly. Serve and enjoy!

Serving Suggestion:
Serve alongside Broccoli and Bell Peppers from page 149.

Non-Pantry-Staple Grocery List
- 1 lb. frozen boneless, skinless chicken breasts
- 3 cups shredded reduced-fat cheddar cheese

Calories 770
Fat 35 g
Fiber 2 g
Carbs 52 g
Net carbs 50 g
Sodium 914 mg
Sugar 2 g
Protein 61 g

Spiced Lentils with Chicken and Rice

Janelle Reitz, Lancaster, PA

Makes 6 servings
Prep. Time: 10 minutes ⚜ Cooking Time: 15 minutes ⚜ Setting: Sauté and Manual
Pressure: High ⚜ Release: Natural then Manual

1 tablespoon olive oil

3-inch cinnamon stick

¾ teaspoon ground cumin

6 garlic cloves, minced

1 onion, sliced

¾ lb. boneless, skinless chicken breast, cubed

1 cup uncooked brown rice, rinsed

½ cup brown lentils, rinsed

1 teaspoon ground cardamom

2½ cups low-sodium, fat-free chicken broth

½ cup raisins

2 tablespoons chopped fresh cilantro

½ cup toasted almonds, *optional*

1. Set the Instant Pot to the Sauté function and heat the oil.

2. Sauté the cinnamon stick, cumin, and garlic for 2 minutes.

3. Add the onion and sauté until tender, about 3 to 5 minutes.

4. Press Cancel. Add the chicken, brown rice, lentils, and cardamom, in that order. Pour in the chicken broth. Do not stir.

5. Secure the lid and set the vent to sealing.

6. Manually set the cook time for 15 minutes on high pressure.

7. When the cooking time is over, let the pressure release naturally for 15 minutes, then manually release the remaining pressure.

8. When the pin drops, remove the lid. Remove the cinnamon stick. Add the raisins, cilantro, and almonds (if using).

TIP

You may replace the olive oil with canola or grapeseed oil if you wish.

Non-Pantry-Staple Grocery List
- 3-inch cinnamon stick
- ¾ lb. boneless, skinless chicken breast
- ½ cup brown lentils
- 1 teaspoon ground cardamom
- ½ cup raisins
- 2 tablespoons chopped fresh cilantro
- ½ cup toasted almonds, *optional*

Calories 329
Fat 7 g
Fiber 2 g
Carbs 41 g
Net carbs 39 g
Sodium 193 mg
Sugar 10 g
Protein 25 g

Chicken Casablanca

Joyce Kaut, Rochester, NY

Makes 8 servings
Prep. Time: 20 minutes ♣ Cooking Time: 12 minutes ♣ Setting: Sauté and Manual
Pressure: High ♣ Release: Natural then Manual

2 tablespoons canola oil, *divided*

2 large onions, sliced

1 teaspoon ground ginger

3 garlic cloves, minced

3 lb. boneless, skinless chicken breasts, cut into bite-size pieces

3 large carrots, diced

½ teaspoon ground cumin

½ teaspoon salt

½ teaspoon pepper

¼ teaspoon cinnamon

2 tablespoons raisins

14.5-ounce can reduced-sodium diced tomatoes

3 small zucchini, sliced

15-ounce can garbanzo beans, drained

2 tablespoons chopped parsley

1. Using the Sauté function of the Instant Pot, heat 1 tablespoon of the oil. Cook the onions, ginger, and garlic for 5 minutes, stirring constantly. Remove the onions, ginger, and garlic from the pot and set aside.

2. Brown the chicken pieces with the remaining oil, then add the cooked onions, ginger, and garlic back in as well as all of the remaining ingredients, except the parsley. Press Cancel.

3. Secure the lid and make sure vent is in the sealing position. Cook on Manual mode for 12 minutes.

4. When the cooking time is over, let the pressure release naturally for 5 minutes and then release the rest of the pressure manually.

5. Garnish with the parsley.

TIP
You may replace the canola oil with olive or grapeseed oil if you wish.

Non-Pantry-Staple Grocery List
- 3 lb. boneless, skinless chicken breasts
- 3 large carrots
- 2 tablespoons raisins
- 14.5-ounce can reduced-sodium diced tomatoes
- 3 small zucchini
- 15-ounce can garbanzo beans
- 2 tablespoons chopped parsley

Calories 419
Fat 11 g
Fiber 4 g
Carbs 17 g
Net carbs 13 g
Sodium 500 mg
Sugar 6 g
Protein 60 g

Lemon Pepper Tilapia

Karen Ceneviva, New Haven, CT

Makes 4 servings
Prep. Time: 1 minute ⚶ Cooking Time: 2–4 minutes ⚶ Setting: Manual
Pressure: High ⚶ Release: Manual

1 cup water

4 (6-ounce) tilapia fillets, fresh or frozen

2 teaspoons lemon pepper seasoning

1. Pour the water into the inner pot of the Instant Pot.

2. Sprinkle the fillets with lemon pepper seasoning on both sides.

3. Place the steamer basket into the inner pot and carefully arrange the tilapia in the basket.

4. Secure the lid and set the vent to sealing.

5. Manually set the cook time for 2 minutes on high pressure for fresh fish, or 4 minutes for frozen fish.

6. When the cooking time is over, manually release the pressure.

7. When the pin drops, remove the lid. Make sure the fish is at 145 degrees.

Serving Suggestion:

Serve with Lemon Curry Rice Mix from page 159.

Non-Pantry-Staple Grocery List
- 4 (6-ounce) tilapia fillets, fresh or frozen
- 2 teaspoons lemon pepper seasoning

Calories 163
Fat 3 g
Fiber 0 g
Carbs 0 g
Net carbs 0 g
Sodium 248 mg
Sugar 0 g
Protein 34 g

Italian Chicken and Broccoli

Liz Clapper, Lancaster, PA

Makes 6 servings
Prep. Time: 15 minutes ☙ Cooking Time: 5 minutes ☙ Setting: Sauté and Manual
Pressure: High ☙ Release: Natural and Manual

1 tablespoon olive oil

1 head broccoli, chopped into florets (about 4 cups)

2 garlic cloves, finely chopped

1 lb. chicken tenderloins

4 medium carrots, sliced thin

2 cups uncooked whole-grain macaroni pasta

3 cups low-fat, low-sodium chicken broth

1 ½ tablespoons Italian seasoning

¼ cup shredded reduced-fat Parmesan cheese

TIP
You may replace the olive oil with canola or grapeseed oil if you wish.

1. Set the Instant Pot to Sauté and heat the oil.

2. Sauté the broccoli for 5 minutes in the inner pot. Set it aside in a bowl and cover to keep warm.

3. Add the garlic and chicken and sauté for 8 minutes.

4. Press Cancel. Add the carrots and stir. Pour the macaroni evenly over the top. Pour in the broth and Italian seasoning. Do not stir.

5. Secure the lid and set the vent to sealing.

6. Manually set the cook time for 5 minutes on high pressure.

7. When the cooking time is over, let the pressure release naturally for 5 minutes, then manually release the remaining pressure.

8. When the pin drops, remove the lid, sprinkle the contents with Parmesan, and serve immediately.

Non-Pantry-Staple Grocery List
- 1 head broccoli
- 1 lb. chicken tenderloins
- 4 medium carrots
- 2 cups whole-grain macaroni pasta
- ¼ cup shredded reduced-fat Parmesan cheese

Calories 298
Fat 9 g
Fiber 4 g
Carbs 23 g
Net carbs 19 g
Sodium 327 mg
Sugar 5 g
Protein 32 g

Main Dishes ❧ **125**

Turkey Meat Loaf

Delores A. Gnagey, Saginaw, MI

Makes 4–5 servings
Prep. Time: 15 minutes ❧ Cooking Time: 15 minutes ❧ Setting: Manual
Pressure: High ❧ Release: Natural ❧ Standing Time: 10 minutes

1 cup plus 1 tablespoon water, *divided*

1 lb. lean ground turkey

½ small onion, minced

1½ tablespoons minced fresh parsley

2 egg whites

2 tablespoons skim milk

½ teaspoon dry mustard

¼ teaspoon salt

⅛ teaspoon ground white pepper

Pinch nutmeg

1 slice whole wheat bread, lightly toasted, made into coarse crumbs

1 tablespoon low-sugar ketchup

1. Set the trivet inside the inner pot of the Instant Pot and pour in 1 cup water.

2. In a medium bowl, mix the ground turkey, onion, and parsley. Set aside.

3. In another bowl, whisk the egg whites. Add the milk, mustard, salt, pepper, and nutmeg to the egg. Whisk to blend.

4. Add the bread crumbs to the egg mixture. Let rest 10 minutes.

5. Add the egg mixture to the meat mixture and blend well.

6. Spray the inside of a 7-inch springform baking pan, then spread the meat mixture into it.

7. Blend together the ketchup and 1 tablespoon water in a small bowl. Spread the mixture on top of the meat. Cover the pan with aluminum foil.

Non-Pantry-Staple Grocery List
- 1 lb. lean ground turkey
- 1½ tablespoons fresh minced parsley
- ½ teaspoon dry mustard
- ⅛ teaspoon ground white pepper
- 1 slice whole wheat bread
- 1 tablespoon low-sugar ketchup

Calories 141
Fat 1.5 g
Fiber 1 g
Carbs 7 g
Net carbs 6 g
Sodium 271 mg
Sugar 2 g
Protein 24 g

8. Place the springform pan on top of the trivet inside the inner pot.

9. Secure the lid and set the vent to sealing.

10. Manually set the cook time for 15 minutes on high pressure.

11. When the cooking time is over, let the pressure release naturally.

12. When the pin drops, remove the lid and use oven mitts to carefully remove the trivet from the inner pot.

13. Allow the meat to stand 10 minutes before slicing to serve.

Serving Suggestion:
Serve with Cauliflower Mashed Potatoes from page 147.

Herbed Fish Fillets

Patricia Howard, Green Valley, AZ

Makes 4 servings
Prep. Time: 5 minutes ♣ Cooking Time: 5–9 minutes ♣ Setting: Manual
Pressure: High ♣ Release: Manual

1 cup water

4 fish fillets (hake, cod, or mahi-mahi), fresh or frozen

Juice of ½ lemon

1 teaspoon dill weed

1 teaspoon dried basil

1 teaspoon no-salt seasoning

1½ teaspoons parsley flakes

4 thin slices lemon

1. Pour the water into the inner pot of the Instant Pot and place the trivet on top.

2. Arrange the fillets in a 7-inch round baking pan. It's all right if they overlap a bit.

3. In a small bowl, mix the lemon juice, dill, basil, no-salt seasoning, and parsley. Pour this over the fillets and place a slice of lemon on top of each fillet.

4. Secure the lid and set the vent to sealing.

5. Manually set the cook time for 5 minutes on high pressure for fresh fish, or 9 minutes for frozen fish.

6. When the cooking time is over, manually release the pressure.

7. When the pin drops, remove the lid. Make sure the fish is at 145 degrees.

Serving Suggestion:

Serve with Herbed Rice Pilaf from page 155.

Non-Pantry-Staple Grocery List
- 4 hake, cod, or mahi-mahi fish fillets, fresh or frozen
- 1 teaspoon dill weed
- 1 teaspoon no-salt seasoning
- 1½ lemons

Calories 99
Fat 1 g
Fiber 0.5 g
Carbs 2 g
Net carbs 1.5 g
Sodium 62 mg
Sugar 0.5 g
Protein 20 g

Greek-Style Halibut Steaks

Kristi See, Weskan, KS

Makes 4 servings
Prep. Time: 10 minutes ☙ Cooking Time: 3 minutes ☙ Setting: Sauté and Manual
Pressure: High ☙ Release: Manual

1 teaspoon olive oil

1 cup unpeeled diced zucchini

$\frac{1}{2}$ cup minced onion

1 garlic clove, peeled and minced

2 cups diced fresh tomatoes

2 tablespoons chopped fresh basil

$\frac{1}{4}$ teaspoon salt

$\frac{1}{4}$ teaspoon pepper

4 (6-ounce) halibut steaks

$\frac{1}{3}$ cup crumbled reduced-fat feta cheese

1 cup water

Serving Suggestion:
Serve with Golden Millet from page 168.

1. Set the Instant Pot to the Sauté function and heat the olive oil in the inner pot.

2. Sauté the zucchini, onion, and garlic for 5 minutes.

3. Mix in the tomatoes, basil, salt, and pepper. Press Cancel.

4. In a 7-inch round baking pan, arrange the halibut steaks. Using oven mitts, carefully pour the zucchini mixture from the inner pot over the halibut. Top with the feta cheese.

5. Quickly wipe out the inner pot. Pour in the water and place the trivet on top.

6. Place the baking pan on top of the trivet in the inner pot. Secure the lid and set the vent to sealing.

7. Manually set the cook time for 3 minutes on high pressure.

8. When the cooking time is over, manually release the pressure.

9. When the pin drops, remove the lid and carefully take the trivet out with oven mitts. Make sure the fish has reached 145°F. Serve halibut and enjoy!

Non-Pantry-Staple Grocery List
- 1 cup diced zucchini
- 2 cups diced fresh tomatoes
- 2 tablespoons chopped fresh basil
- 4 (6-ounce) halibut steaks
- $\frac{1}{3}$ cup crumbled reduced-fat feta cheese

Calories 248

Fat 7 g

Fiber 2 g

Carbs 7 g

Net carbs 5 g

Sodium 343 mg

Sugar 4 g

Protein 40 g

TIP
You may replace the olive oil with canola or grapeseed oil if you wish.

Simple Salmon

Evie Hershey, Atglen, PA

Makes 4 servings
Prep. Time: 3 minutes ⚹ Cooking Time: 3–5 minutes ⚹ Setting: Manual
Pressure: High ⚹ Release: Manual

1 cup water

1 teaspoon olive oil

1 lb. salmon fillet, fresh or frozen

½ teaspoon Old Bay seasoning

½ teaspoon fine bread crumbs

Serving Suggestion:
Serve with Vegetable Medley from page 153.

1. Pour the water into the inner pot of the Instant Pot. Place the trivet on top.

2. In a 7-inch round baking pan, spread the olive oil on the bottom.

3. Season the salmon fillet with the Old Bay seasoning and place it skin-side down in the baking pan. Sprinkle the bread crumbs on top.

4. Place the baking pan on top of the trivet in the inner pot.

5. Secure the lid and set the vent to sealing.

6. Manually set the cook time on high pressure for 3 minutes if fresh or 5 minutes if frozen.

7. When the cooking time is over, manually release the pressure.

8. When the pin drops, remove the lid and carefully remove the trivet from the inner pot with oven mitts. Check to make sure the fillet is at 145 degrees.

Non-Pantry-Staple Grocery List
- 1 lb. salmon fillet, fresh or frozen
- ½ teaspoon Old Bay seasoning
- ½ teaspoon fine bread crumbs

Calories 229
Fat 17 g
Fiber 1 g
Carbs 10 g
Net carbs 9 g
Sodium 245 mg
Sugar 1 g
Protein 25 g

TIP
You may replace the olive oil with canola or grapeseed oil if you wish.

Salmon with Chives

Gloria Julien, Gladstone, MI

Makes 2 servings
Prep. Time: 5 minutes ⚘ Cooking Time: 3–5 minutes ⚘ Setting: Manual
Pressure: High ⚘ Release: Manual

1 cup water
2 (5-ounce) pieces salmon with skin
2 teaspoons extra-virgin olive oil
1 tablespoon chopped chives
1 tablespoon fresh tarragon leaves, *optional*

TIP
You may replace the olive oil with canola or grapeseed oil if you wish.

Non-Pantry-Staple Grocery List
- 2 (5-ounce) pieces salmon
- 1 tablespoon chopped chives
- 1 tablespoon fresh tarragon leaves, *optional*

Calories 341
Fat 23 g
Fiber 0 g
Carbs 1 g
Net carbs 1 g
Sodium 85 mg
Sugar 0 g
Protein 30 g

1. Pour the water into the inner pot of the Instant Pot and place the trivet on top.

2. Line a 7-inch round baking pan with foil.

3. Rub the salmon all over with the oil.

4. Place the salmon skin-side down on the foil. Place the baking pan on top of the trivet in the inner pot.

5. Secure the lid and set the vent to sealing.

6. Manually set the cook time on high pressure for 3 minutes if fresh or 5 minutes if frozen.

7. When the cooking time is over, manually release the pressure.

8. When the pin drops, remove the lid and carefully remove the trivet from the inner pot with oven mitts. Check to make sure the fillet is at 145 degrees.

9. Using a metal spatula, lift salmon off skin and place salmon on serving plate. Discard skin.

10. Sprinkle salmon with herbs and serve.

Serving Suggestion:
Serve with Artichokes and Brown Rice from page 160.

Wild Salmon with Capers

Bernita Boyts, Shawnee Mission, KS

Makes 4 servings

Prep. Time: 15 minutes ☙ Cooking Time: 3–5 minutes ☙ Setting: Manual and Sauté
Pressure: High ☙ Release: Manual

1 cup water

1 teaspoon olive oil

1 lb. wild salmon fillet

Salt to taste

Black pepper to taste

2 tablespoons butter or margarine

1 garlic clove, chopped fine

$\frac{1}{4}$ cup white wine or water

2 tablespoons capers

2 scallions, finely chopped

1 teaspoon fresh dill weed

1 medium tomato, chopped

1 tablespoon lemon juice

TIP

You may replace the olive oil with canola or grapeseed oil if you wish.

1. Pour the water into the inner pot of the Instant Pot. Place the trivet on top.

2. In a 7-inch round baking pan, spread the olive oil on the bottom.

3. Season the salmon fillet with salt and pepper and lay it skin-side down in the baking pan.

4. Place the baking pan on top of the trivet in the inner pot.

5. Secure the lid and set the vent to sealing.

6. Manually set the cook time on high pressure for 3 minutes if fresh or 5 minutes if frozen.

7. When the cooking time is over, manually release the pressure. Press Cancel.

8. When the pin drops, remove the lid and carefully remove the trivet from the inner pot with oven mitts. Check to make sure the fillet is at 145 degrees. Cover the fish to keep it warm.

Non-Pantry-Staple Grocery List
- 1 lb. wild salmon fillet
- $\frac{1}{4}$ cup white wine, *optional as you may use water instead*
- 2 tablespoons capers
- 2 scallions
- 1 teaspoon fresh dill weed
- 1 medium tomato
- 1 tablespoon lemon juice

Calories 318

Fat 22 g

Fiber 0.5 g

Carbs 3 g

Net carbs 2.5 g

Sodium 228 mg

Sugar 1 g

Protein 24 g

9. Carefully pour the water out of the inner pot and quickly wipe dry.

10. Set the Instant Pot to Sauté and melt the butter in the inner pot. Add the garlic. Stir and cook for about 30 seconds.

11. Add the wine and heat until bubbling, scraping brown bits into liquid.

12. Add the capers, scallions, and dill. Cook for another minute.

13. Stir in the chopped tomato. Heat through.

14. Sprinkle the lemon juice over the salmon. Top with the sauce and serve.

Serving Suggestion:
Serve with Broccoli with Garlic from page 148.

Maple-Glazed Salmon

Jenelle Miller, Marion, SD

Makes 6 servings
Prep. Time: 5 minutes ⚘ Cooking Time: 3 minutes ⚘ Setting: Manual
Pressure: High ⚘ Release: Manual

2 teaspoons paprika

2 teaspoons chili powder

½ teaspoon ground cumin

½ teaspoon brown sugar

½ teaspoon kosher salt

6 (4-ounce) salmon fillets

Nonstick cooking spray

1 tablespoon maple syrup

1 cup water

1. In a small bowl, combine the first five ingredients.

2. Rub the fillets with the seasoning mixture.

3. Spray a 7-inch round baking pan with nonstick cooking spray, and place the salmon in the pan skin-side down. Drizzle the fish with the maple syrup.

4. Pour the water into the inner pot of the Instant Pot and place the trivet on top.

5. Secure the lid and set the vent to sealing.

6. Manually set the cook time for 3 minutes on high pressure.

7. When the cooking time is over, manually release the pressure.

8. When the pin drops, remove the lid and carefully remove the trivet from the inner pot with oven mitts.

Check to make sure the fillets are at 145 degrees.

Non-Pantry-Staple Grocery List
• 6 (4-ounce) salmon fillets

Calories 250
Fat 15 g
Fiber 0.5 g
Carbs 3 g
Net carbs 2.5 g
Sodium 253 mg
Sugar 2 g
Protein 23 g

Caesar Salmon Fillets

Gloria D. Good, Harrisonburg, VA

Makes 6 servings
Prep. Time: 8 minutes ⚬ Marinade Time: 2 hours ⚬ Cooking Time: 3 minutes
Setting: Manual ⚬ Pressure: High ⚬ Release: Manual

6 (4-ounce) salmon fillets
½ cup fat-free Caesar salad dressing
Nonstick cooking spray
1½ tablespoons reduced-sodium soy sauce or tamari
1 garlic clove, minced
1 cup water

Non-Pantry-Staple Grocery List
- 6 (4-ounce) salmon fillets
- ½ cup fat-free Caesar salad dressing
- 1½ tablespoons reduced-sodium soy sauce or tamari

Calories 318
Fat 24 g
Fiber 0 g
Carbs 1 g
Net carbs 1 g
Sodium 447 mg
Sugar 0 g
Protein 24 g

1. Place the fillets in a plastic bag. Add the salad dressing. Seal bag and turn to coat.

2. Refrigerate for at least 2 hours.

3. Drain and discard marinade.

4. Spray a 7-inch round baking pan with nonstick cooking spray, and place the salmon in the pan skin-side down.

5. In a shallow bowl, combine the soy sauce and garlic. Brush over the salmon.

6. Pour the water into the inner pot of the Instant Pot and place the trivet on top. Place the baking pan on top of the trivet.

7. Secure the lid and set the vent to sealing.

8. Manually set the cook time for 3 minutes on high pressure.

9. When the cooking time is over, manually release the pressure.

10. When the pin drops, remove the lid and carefully remove the trivet from the inner pot with oven mitts. Check to make sure the fillets are at 145 degrees.

Serving Suggestion:
Serve with Bulgur Pilaf from page 164.

Side Dishes

Fresh Zucchini and Tomatoes

Pauline Morrison, St. Marys, Ontario

Makes 6–8 servings
Prep. Time: 8 minutes ❧ Cooking Time: 2 minutes ❧ Setting: Manual and Sauté
Pressure: High ❧ Release: Manual

1 cup water

1½ lb. zucchini, peeled if you wish, and cut into ¼-inch slices

1½ tablespoons coconut oil

1½ garlic cloves, minced

19-ounce can low-sodium stewed tomatoes, broken up

½ teaspoon salt

TIP
You may replace the coconut oil with olive oil or canola oil if you wish.

1. Pour the water into the inner pot of the Instant Pot and place the steaming basket in the inner pot. Place the zucchini slices in the basket.

2. Secure the lid and set the vent to sealing.

3. Manually set the cook time for 2 minutes on high pressure.

4. When the cooking time is over, manually release the pressure.

5. When the pin drops, remove the lid and the steaming basket. Press Cancel.

6. Drain the water carefully from the inner pot and wipe dry.

7. Press Sauté and heat the coconut oil in the inner pot. When the oil is heated, sauté the garlic for 1 minute.

8. Add the tomatoes with their juices, garlic, salt, and zucchini. Mix well and let all the ingredients heat through, about 3 to 5 minutes.

Non-Pantry-Staple Grocery List
- 1½ lb. zucchini
- 19-ounce can low-sodium stewed tomatoes

Calories 91
Fat 5 g
Fiber 2 g
Carbs 12 g
Net carbs 10 g
Sodium 433 mg
Sugar 4 g
Protein 2 g

Instant Spaghetti Squash

Hope Comerford, Clinton Township, MI

Makes 4–6 servings
Prep. Time: 5 minutes ❧ Cooking Time: 10 minutes ❧ Setting: Manual
Pressure: High ❧ Release: Manual

1 medium spaghetti squash
1 cup water

1. Cut the spaghetti squash in the middle (not lengthwise) so that it will fit in the inner pot.

2. Pour the water into the inner pot of the Instant Pot and place the trivet on top.

3. Place the squash pieces, cut-side down, on the trivet.

4. Secure the lid and set the vent to sealing.

5. Manually set the cook time for 10 minutes on high pressure.

6. When the cooking time is over, manually release the pressure.

7. When the pin drops, remove the lid.

8. Carefully remove the squash, and, using a fork, shred the squash inside the skin. To do this, move your fork clockwise around the inside of the squash.

Serving Suggestions:
Serve with a little bit of butter or margarine and a touch of salt and pepper.

Spaghetti squash is a delicious and healthy alternative to traditional spaghetti noodles.

Non-Pantry-Staple Grocery List
- 1 medium spaghetti squash

Calories 16
Fat 0 g
Fiber 1 g
Carbs 3 g
Net carbs 2 g
Sodium 9 mg
Sugar 1 g
Protein 0 g

Squash Apple Bake

Lavina Hochstedler, Grand Blanc, MI

Makes 8 servings
Prep. Time: 10 minutes ⚭ Cooking Time: 5 minutes ⚭ Setting: Manual
Pressure: High ⚭ Release: Natural then Manual

3 cups cubed butternut squash, *divided*

2½ tablespoons honey or brown sugar

¼ cup orange juice or apple juice

1½ teaspoons cornstarch

2 apples, cut in short thick slices, *divided*

3 tablespoons raisins, *divided*

¾ teaspoon cinnamon

3 teaspoons soft margarine, non-hydrogenated

1 cup water

Non-Pantry-Staple Grocery List
- 3 cups cubed butternut squash
- 2 apples
- 3 tablespoons raisins

Calories 95
Fat 1.5 g
Fiber 2 g
Carbs 21 g
Net carbs 19 g
Sodium 20 mg
Sugar 14 g
Protein 1 g

1. Slice the butternut squash into ¾-inch rounds. Peel and cut into cubes.

2. In a small bowl, combine the honey, juice, and cornstarch.

3. In a greased 7-inch round baking dish, layer in half the squash, followed by a layer of half the apples, and then a layer of half the raisins.

4. Repeat layers.

5. Sprinkle with the cinnamon.

6. Pour juice mixture over all.

7. Dot with the margarine.

8. Pour the water into the inner pot of the Instant Pot and place the trivet on top.

9. Place the baking dish on top of the trivet. Secure the lid and set the vent to sealing.

10. Manually set the cook time for 5 minutes on high pressure.

11. When the cooking time is over, let the pressure release naturally for 15 minutes, then manually release the remaining pressure.

Seasoned Beets

Hope Comerford, Clinton Township, MI

Makes 4–6 servings
Prep. Time: 15 minutes ☙ Cooking Time: 10 minutes ☙ Setting: Manual
Pressure: High ☙ Release: Natural then Manual

4–6 large beets, scrubbed well and tops removed

3 tablespoons olive oil

1 teaspoon sea salt

¼ teaspoon pepper

3 tablespoons balsamic vinegar

1 tablespoon lemon juice

1 cup water

TIP
You may replace the olive oil with coconut, canola, or grapeseed oil if you wish.

Non-Pantry-Staple Grocery List
- 4–6 large beets
- 3 tablespoons balsamic vinegar
- 1 tablespoon lemon juice

1. Use foil to make a packet around each beet.

2. Divide the olive oil, salt, pepper, balsamic vinegar, and lemon juice evenly between each packet.

3. Pour the water into the inner pot of the Instant Pot and place the trivet or steamer basket on top.

4. Place each beet packet onto the trivet or into the steamer basket.

5. Secure the lid and set the vent to sealing.

6. Manually set the cook time for 16 minutes on high pressure.

7. When the cooking time is over, let the pressure release naturally for 10 minutes, then manually release the remaining pressure.

8. When the pin drops, remove the lid. Transfer the beets to a plate using tongs. Allow to cool and let the steam escape.

9. Once cool enough to handle, unwrap each beet packet and use a paring knife to gently peel the skin off each beet. Cut into bite-size pieces and serve with juice from the packet over the top.

Calories 99
Fat 7 g
Fiber 2 g
Carbs 8 g
Net carbs 6 g
Sodium 314 mg
Sugar 6 g
Protein 1 g

Perfect Sweet Potatoes

Brittney Horst, Lititz, PA

Makes 4–6 servings
Prep. Time: 5 minutes   ♣   Cooking Time: 15 minutes   ♣   Setting: Manual
Pressure: High   ♣   Release: Natural

4–6 medium sweet potatoes

1 cup water

1. Scrub the skin of the sweet potatoes with a brush until clean. Pour the water into the inner pot of the Instant Pot. Place the steamer basket in the bottom of the inner pot. Place the sweet potatoes on top of the steamer basket.

2. Secure the lid and turn the valve to seal.

3. Select the Manual mode and set to pressure cook on high for 15 minutes.

4. Allow pressure to release naturally (about 10 minutes).

5. Once the pressure valve lowers, remove the lid and serve immediately.

Non-Pantry-Staple Grocery List
- 4–6 sweet potatoes

TIPS

1. You may also use a trivet if you do not have a steamer basket.

2. You can store cooked sweet potatoes in the refrigerator for 3 to 4 days in an airtight container.

3. Superlarge sweet potatoes need more than 15 minutes! I tried one mega sweet potato, and it was not cooked in the center. Maybe 20 minutes will do.

Calories 130
Fat 0 g
Fiber 4 g
Carbs 26 g
Net carbs 22 g
Sodium 72 mg
Sugar 5 g
Protein 2 g

Cauliflower Mashed Potatoes

Anne Hummel, Millersburg, OH

Makes 4 servings
Prep. Time: 10 minutes ⚭ Cooking Time: 3 minutes ⚭ Setting: Manual
Pressure: High ⚭ Release: Manual

1 head cauliflower

1 cup water

1 garlic clove

1 leek, white part only, split into 4 pieces

1 tablespoon soft margarine, non-hydrogenated

Pepper to taste

1. Remove the core and break the cauliflower into smaller florets, or roughly chop it.

2. Pour the water into the inner pot of the Instant Pot and place the steamer basket in as well.

3. Put the cauliflower, garlic, and leek into the steamer basket. Secure the lid and set the vent to sealing.

4. Manually set the cook time for 3 minutes on high pressure.

5. When the cooking time is over, manually release the pressure. Remove the steamer basket carefully.

6. While the vegetables are hot, puree them until the vegetables resemble mashed potatoes. (Use a food processor, or, if you prefer a smoother texture, use a blender. Process only a small portion at a time, holding the blender lid on firmly with a tea towel.) You can also mash these vegetables by hand if you prefer a "chunkier" texture.

7. Add a little hot water if vegetables seem dry.

8. Stir in margarine and pepper to taste.

Non-Pantry-Staple Grocery List
- 1 head cauliflower
- 1 leek

Calories 59
Fat 3 g
Fiber 2 g
Carbs 7 g
Net carbs 5 g
Sodium 60 mg
Sugar 2 g
Protein 2 g

Broccoli with Garlic

Andrea Cunningham, Arlington, KS

Makes 4 servings
Prep. Time: 5 minutes ❧ Cooking Time: 0 minutes ❧ Setting: Manual
Pressure: High and Sauté ❧ Release: Manual

½ cup cold water

1 head (about 5 cups) broccoli, cut into long pieces all the way through (you will eat the stems)

1 tablespoon olive oil

2–3 garlic cloves, sliced thin

⅛ teaspoon pepper

Lemon wedges, to taste

TIP
You may replace the olive oil with canola or grapeseed oil if you wish.

Non-Pantry-Staple Grocery List
- 1 head broccoli
- ½ lemon

1. Place a steamer basket into the inner pot along with the ½ cup cold water. Put the broccoli into the steamer basket.

2. Secure the lid and set the vent to sealing.

3. Manually set the cook time for 0 minutes on high pressure.

4. Manually release the pressure when it's done. Press Cancel.

5. When the pin drops, open the lid and place the broccoli into an ice bath or run under cold water to stop it from cooking. Let it air dry.

6. Carefully remove the water from the inner pot and wipe it dry.

7. Set the Instant Pot to the Sauté function and heat the oil.

8. Sauté the garlic for 1 minute, then add the broccoli, sprinkle it with the pepper, and continue to sauté for an additional 1 to 2 minutes.

9. Just before serving, squeeze lemon juice over the top.

Calories 55
Fat 4 g
Fiber 2 g
Carbs 5 g
Net carbs 3 g
Sodium 23 mg
Sugar 1 g
Protein 2 g

Broccoli and Bell Peppers

Frieda Weisz, Aberdeen, SD

Makes 8 servings
Prep. Time: 10 minutes ✦ Cooking Time: 0 minutes ✦ Setting: Manual
Pressure: High and Sauté ✦ Release: Manual

I cup water

2 lb. fresh broccoli, trimmed and chopped into bite-size pieces

I tablespoon olive oil

I onion, peeled and cut into slices

I garlic clove, minced

I green or red bell pepper, cut into thin slices

4 tablespoons low-sodium gluten-free soy sauce or Bragg's Liquid Aminos

½ teaspoon salt

Dash black pepper

I tablespoon sesame seeds for garnish, *optional*

Non-Pantry-Staple Grocery List
- 2 lb. fresh broccoli
- I green or red bell pepper
- 4 tablespoons low-sodium gluten-free soy sauce or Bragg's Liquid Aminos
- I tablespoon sesame seeds, *optional*

Calories 34
Fat 2 g
Fiber 1 g
Carbs 4 g
Net carbs 3 g
Sodium 460 mg
Sugar 1 g
Protein 2 g

1. Place a steamer basket into the inner pot along with the water. Put the broccoli into the steamer basket.

2. Secure the lid and set the vent to sealing.

3. Manually set the cook time for 0 minutes on high pressure.

4. Manually release the pressure when it's done. Press Cancel.

5. When the pin drops, open the lid and place the broccoli into an ice bath or run under cold water to stop it from cooking. Let it air dry.

6. Carefully remove the water from the inner pot and wipe it dry.

7. Set the Instant Pot to the Sauté function and heat the oil.

8. Sauté the onion and garlic for 3 minutes, then add the bell pepper and sauté another 3 minutes or so.

9. Add the broccoli, soy sauce, salt, and pepper, and continue to sauté for an additional 1 to 2 minutes.

10. Sprinkle with the sesame seeds, if using.

TIP
Feel free to add other veggies, such as celery, if you have them on hand. Season with fresh herbs and red pepper flakes for more flavor.

Rosemary Carrots

Orpha Herr, Andover, NY

Makes 6 servings
Prep. Time: 10 minutes ⚘ Cooking Time: 2 minutes ⚘ Setting: Manual and Sauté
Pressure: High ⚘ Release: Manual

1 cup water
1½ lb. carrots, sliced
1 tablespoon olive oil
½ cup diced green bell pepper
1 teaspoon dried rosemary, crushed
¼ teaspoon coarsely ground black pepper

TIP
You may replace the olive oil with coconut, canola, or grapeseed oil if you wish.

Non-Pantry-Staple Grocery List
- 1½ lb. carrots
- ½ cup diced green bell pepper
- 1 teaspoon dried rosemary

1. Pour the water into the inner pot of the Instant Pot, place the sliced carrots into a steamer basket, and put the steamer basket into the inner pot.

2. Secure the lid and set the vent to sealing.

3. Manually set the cook time for 2 minutes on high pressure.

4. When the cooking time is over, manually release the pressure. Wait for the pin to drop and remove the lid. Press Cancel.

5. Carefully remove the carrots, set aside, and empty the water out of the inner pot. Wipe dry.

6. Place the inner pot back into the Instant Pot, then press Sauté and heat the oil in the inner pot.

7. Add the green bell pepper and sauté for 5 minutes, then add the carrots and stir.

8. Sprinkle the carrots and green pepper with rosemary and black pepper. Serve and enjoy!

Calories 70
Fat 2.5 g
Fiber 3 g
Carbs 12 g
Net carbs 9 g
Sodium 79 mg
Sugar 6 g
Protein 1 g

Orange-Glazed Parsnips

Sandra Haverstraw, Hummelstown, PA

Makes 6 servings
Prep. Time: 5 minutes ❧ Cooking Time: 2 minutes ❧ Setting: Manual and Sauté
Pressure: High ❧ Release: Manual

4½ cups ½-inch parsnip slices

1 cup water

2 tablespoons soft margarine, non-hydrogenated

1 tablespoon honey

¼ cup orange juice

1 tablespoon grated orange zest

¼ teaspoon nutmeg

Non-Pantry-Staple Grocery List
- 4½ cups ½-inch parsnip slices
- ¼ cup orange juice
- 1 tablespoon grated orange peel

1. Place the parsnips into a steamer basket, then place the steamer basket into the inner pot of the Instant Pot along with the water.

2. Secure the lid and set the vent to sealing.

3. Manually set the cook time for 2 minutes on high pressure.

4. When the cooking time is over, manually release the pressure. Press Cancel.

5. When the pin drops, remove the lid. Remove the parsnips and set aside. Carefully drain the water from the inner pot and wipe the inner pot dry.

6. Press Sauté and add the parsnips back into the inner pot along with the margarine, honey, orange juice, orange zest, and nutmeg. Stir and sauté for about 2 to 3 minutes.

7. Serve hot.

Serving Suggestion:

These parsnips are especially good with turkey or pork. You can also use the orange glaze over cooked, cubed winter squash or sweet potatoes.

Calories 124
Fat 4 g
Fiber 5 g
Carbs 22 g
Net carbs 117 g
Sodium 55 mg
Sugar 9 g
Protein 1 g

Vegetable Medley

Teena Wagner, Waterloo, ON

Makes 8 servings
Prep. Time: 20 minutes ⚜ Cooking Time: 2 minutes ⚜ Setting: Manual and Sauté
Pressure: High ⚜ Release: Manual

2 medium parsnips

4 medium carrots

1 turnip, about 4½ inches diameter

1 cup water

1 teaspoon salt

3 tablespoons turbinado sugar, or sugar of your choice

2 tablespoons canola or olive oil

½ teaspoon salt

TIP
You may replace the oil with coconut, or grapeseed oil if you wish.

1. Clean and peel the vegetables. Cut into 1-inch pieces.

2. Place the water and salt into the inner pot of the Instant Pot with the vegetables.

3. Secure the lid and make sure vent is set to sealing. Press Manual and set for 2 minutes.

4. When the cooking time is over, release the pressure manually and press Cancel. Drain the water from the inner pot.

5. Press Sauté, add the vegetables back into the inner pot, and stir in the sugar, oil, and salt. Cook until sugar is dissolved. Serve.

Non-Pantry-Staple Grocery List
- 2 medium parsnips
- 4 medium carrots
- 1 turnip, about 4½ inches in diameter

Calories 213
Fat 7 g
Fiber 7 g
Carbs 37 g
Net carbs 30 g
Sodium 351 mg
Sugar 21 g
Protein 2 g

Herbed Rice Pilaf

Betty K. Drescher, Quakertown, PA

Makes 6 servings
Prep. Time: 10 minutes ☙ Cooking Time: 22 minutes ☙ Setting: Sauté and Manual
Pressure: High ☙ Release: Natural

1 tablespoon olive oil

½ cup chopped onion

1 cup chopped celery

1½ cups raw brown rice

1¾ cups low-sodium, fat-free chicken broth

¾ teaspoon Worcestershire sauce

¾ teaspoon low-sodium soy sauce

¾ teaspoon dried oregano

¾ teaspoon dried thyme

TIP
You may replace the olive oil with canola or grapeseed oil if you wish.

1. Set the Instant Pot to the Sauté function and heat the oil in the inner pot.

2. Add the onion and celery to the inner pot and sauté for about 5 minutes. Add the rice and lightly toast, about 1 minute. Press Cancel.

3. Add the broth, Worcestershire sauce, soy sauce, oregano, and thyme. Secure the lid and set the vent to sealing.

4. Manually set the time for 22 minutes on high pressure.

5. When the cooking time is over, let the pressure release naturally.

6. When the pin drops, remove the lid and fluff the rice with a fork. Serve and enjoy!

Non-Pantry-Staple Grocery List
- 1 cup chopped celery
- ¾ teaspoon Worcestershire sauce
- ¾ teaspoon low-sodium soy sauce

Calories 224
Fat 5 g
Fiber 2 g
Carbs 40 g
Net carbs 38 g
Sodium 164 mg
Sugar 2 g
Protein 6 g

Cilantro Lime Rice

Cindy Herren, West Des Moines, IA

Makes 6–8 servings
Prep. Time: 5 minutes   Cooking Time: 3 minutes   Setting: Manual
Pressure: High   Release: Natural

2 cups extra-long grain rice or jasmine rice

4 cup water

2 tablespoons olive oil or butter, *divided*

2 teaspoons salt

¼ cup fresh chopped cilantro

1 lime, juiced

TIP
You may replace the olive oil with canola or grapeseed oil if you wish.

1. Add the rice, the water, 1 tablespoon of the oil, and the salt to the inner pot of the Instant Pot and stir.

2. Secure the lid and set the vent to sealing.

3. Manually set the cook time to 3 minutes on high pressure.

4. When the cooking time is over, let the pressure release naturally for 10 minutes, then manually release the remaining pressure.

5. When the pin drops, remove the lid. Fluff the rice with a fork. Add the chopped cilantro, lime juice, and remaining oil and mix well.

Serving Suggestion:

Serve with Barbacoa Beef (see recipe on page 103).

Non-Pantry-Staple Grocery List
- 2 cups extra-long grain rice or jasmine rice
- 1 lime
- ¼ cup fresh chopped cilantro

Calories 201
Fat 4 g
Fiber 1 g
Carbs 38 g
Net carbs 37 g
Sodium 486 mg
Sugar 0 g
Protein 3 g

Hometown Spanish Rice

Beverly Flatt-Getz, Warriors Mark, PA

Makes 6–8 servings
Prep. Time: 8 minutes ⚘ Cooking Time: 3 minutes ⚘ Setting: Sauté and Manual
Pressure: High ⚘ Release: Natural then Manual

1 tablespoon olive oil

1 large onion, chopped

1 bell pepper, chopped

2 cups long-grain rice, rinsed

1½ cups low-sodium chicken stock

28-ounce can low-sodium stewed tomatoes

Grated Parmesan cheese, *optional*

TIP
You may replace the olive oil with canola or grapeseed oil if you wish.

1. Set the Instant Pot to Sauté and heat the oil in the inner pot.

2. Sauté the onion and bell pepper in the inner pot for about 3 to 5 minutes.

3. Add the rice and continue to sauté for about 1 more minute. Press Cancel.

4. Add the chicken stock and tomatoes with their juices into the inner pot, in that order.

5. Secure the lid and set the vent to sealing.

6. Manually set the cook time for 3 minutes on high pressure.

7. When the cooking time is over, let the pressure release naturally for 10 minutes, then manually release the remaining pressure.

8. When the pin drops, remove the lid. Fluff the rice with a fork.

9. Sprinkle with Parmesan cheese, if using, just before serving.

Non-Pantry-Staple Grocery List
- 1 bell pepper
- 2 cups long-grain rice
- 28-ounce can stewed tomatoes
- Grated Parmesan cheese, *optional*

Calories 284

Fat 5 g

Fiber 3 g

Carbs 53 g

Net carbs 50 g

Sodium 518 mg

Sugar 4 g

Protein 7 g

Lemon Curry Rice Mix

Susan Kasting, Jenks, OK

Makes 8 servings
Prep. Time: 3 minutes ❧ Cooking Time: 15 minutes ❧ Setting: Manual
Pressure: High ❧ Release: Natural

2 cups raw brown rice
1 tablespoon grated lemon peel
½ cup golden raisins
½ cup slivered almonds
2 teaspoons curry powder
½ teaspoon ground white pepper
¼ teaspoon cumin
¼ teaspoon crushed red pepper
2 cups water or low-sodium vegetable stock

1. Place all of the ingredients in the inner pot of the Instant Pot. Secure the lid and set the vent to sealing.

2. Manually set the cook time for 15 minutes on high pressure.

3. When the cooking time is over, let the pressure release naturally for 5 minutes, then manually release the remaining pressure.

4. When the pin drops, remove the lid and fluff the rice with a fork. Serve and enjoy!

Non-Pantry-Staple Grocery List
- 1 tablespoon grated lemon peel
- ½ cup golden raisins
- ½ cup slivered almonds
- 2 teaspoons curry powder
- ½ teaspoon ground white pepper
- ¼ teaspoon crushed red pepper

Calories 244
Fat 5 g
Fiber g
Carbs 46 g
Net carbs 43 g
Sodium 139 mg
Sugar 7 g
Protein 6 g

Artichokes and Brown Rice

Betty K. Drescher, Quakertown, PA

Makes 6 servings
Prep. Time: 5 minutes ❧ Cooking Time: 15 minutes ❧ Setting: Sauté and Manual
Pressure: High ❧ Release: Natural then Manual

1 tablespoon extra-virgin olive oil

14.5-ounce can artichokes, drained and cut into chunks

1 cup raw brown rice

1 cup low-sodium vegetable stock

TIP
You may replace the olive oil with canola or grapeseed oil if you wish.

1. Set the Instant Pot to Sauté and heat the oil in the inner pot.

2. Sauté the artichokes in the olive oil for about 5 minutes. Press cancel.

3. Add the rice and vegetable stock to the inner pot. Secure the lid and set the vent to sealing.

4. Manually set the cook time for 15 minutes on high pressure.

5. When the cooking time is over, let the pressure release naturally for 5 minutes, then manually release the remaining pressure.

6. When the pin drops, remove the lid and fluff the rice with a fork. Serve and enjoy!

Non-Pantry-Staple Grocery List
• 14.5-ounce can artichokes

Calories 165
Fat 3 g
Fiber 5 g
Carbs 31 g
Net carbs 26 g
Sodium 156 mg
Sugar 1 g
Protein 5 g

Apple-Cranberry Wild Rice

Heather Horst, Lebanon, PA

Makes 6 cups
Prep. Time: 5 minutes ♣ Cooking Time: 20 minutes ♣ Setting: Manual
Pressure: High ♣ Release: Natural

½ cup raw brown rice

½ cup raw wild rice

1 teaspoon dried savory

1 small leek (white portion only), coarsely chopped, or 3 tablespoons chopped onion

1 teaspoon olive oil

⅓ cup dried cranberries

¼ cup chopped dried apples

½ teaspoon onion powder

½ teaspoon lemon-pepper seasoning

1½ cups low-sodium vegetable stock

1 cup water

1. Place the ingredients in the inner pot in the order shown. Secure the lid and set the vent to sealing.

2. Manually set the cook time for 20 minutes on high pressure.

3. When the cooking time is over, let the pressure release naturally.

TIP
You may replace the olive oil with coconut, canola, or grapeseed oil if you wish.

Non-Pantry-Staple Grocery List
- ½ cup wild rice
- 1 teaspoon dried savory
- 1 small leek
- ⅓ cup dried cranberries
- ¼ cup chopped dried apples
- ½ teaspoon onion powder
- ½ teaspoon lemon-pepper seasoning

Calories 171
Fat 3 g
Fiber 3 g
Carbs 34 g
Net carbs 31 g
Sodium 169 mg
Sugar 9 g
Protein 4 g

Barbecue Lentils

Sherri Grindle, Goshen, IN

Makes 8 servings
Prep. Time: 10 minutes ❧ Cooking Time: 10–12 minutes ❧ Setting: Manual
Pressure: High ❧ Release: Manual

1 tablespoon extra-virgin olive oil

1 cup chopped red onion

1 tablespoon minced garlic

2 teaspoons chili powder

1 teaspoon dry mustard

3 cups low-sodium chicken stock or vegetable stock

¾ cup low-sodium tomato sauce

3 tablespoons balsamic vinegar

1 tablespoon Dijon mustard

2 tablespoons honey

1½ cups brown lentils, rinsed

Pepper to taste

TIP
You may replace the olive oil with canola or grapeseed oil if you wish.

1. Turn the Instant Pot to Sauté and heat the oil in the inner pot.

2. Add the onion and sauté until soft and translucent, about 3 minutes.

3. Add the garlic, chili powder, and dry mustard. Sauté until fragrant, about 1 minute. Do not brown garlic.

4. Add the stock, tomato sauce, vinegar, mustard, honey, and lentils. Press Cancel.

5. Secure the lid and set the vent to sealing.

6. Manually set the cook time to 10 minutes on high pressure.

7. When the cooking time is over, manually release the pressure.

8. If lentils are not tender enough, reseal the lid, set the vent to sealing, and cook for another 2 minutes.

9. Season with pepper.

Non-Pantry-Staple Grocery List
- 1 teaspoon dry mustard
- ¾ cup low-sodium tomato sauce
- 3 tablespoons balsamic vinegar
- 1 tablespoon Dijon mustard
- 1½ cups brown lentils

Calories 102
Fat 3 g
Fiber 1 g
Carbs 16 g
Net carbs 15 g
Sodium 309 mg
Sugar 10 g
Protein 4 g

Bulgur Pilaf

Mary Kathryn Yoder, Harrisonville, MO

Makes 8 servings
Prep. Time: 15 minutes ⚜ Cooking Time: 12 minutes ⚜ Setting: Manual
Pressure: High ⚜ Release: Manual

1 tablespoon olive oil
1 medium onion chopped
$\frac{1}{2}$ cup chopped celery
1 cup raw bulgur
1 $\frac{1}{2}$ cups low-sodium chicken broth
$\frac{1}{2}$ teaspoon poultry seasoning
$\frac{1}{4}$ cup chopped nuts

1. In the inner pot of the Instant Pot, heat the oil on the Sauté function.

2. Sauté the onion and celery in the olive oil for 5 to 8 minutes.

3. Add the bulgur and sauté 3 more minutes. Press Cancel.

4. Add the broth and seasoning.

5. Secure the lid and set the vent to sealing.

6. Manually set the cook time for 12 minutes on high pressure.

7. When the cooking time is over, manually release the pressure.

8. When the pin drops, remove the lid. Fluff with a fork.

9. Just before serving stir in the chopped nuts.

TIP
You may replace the olive oil with canola or grapeseed oil if you wish.

Non-Pantry-Staple Grocery List
- $\frac{1}{2}$ cup chopped celery
- 1 cup bulgur
- $\frac{1}{2}$ teaspoon poultry seasoning
- $\frac{1}{4}$ cup chopped nuts (of your choice)

Calories 121
Fat 5 g
Fiber 3 g
Carbs 17 g
Net carbs 14 g
Sodium 76 mg
Sugar 1 g
Protein 4 g

Curried Barley

Diann J. Dunham, State College, PA

Makes 6 servings
Prep. Time: 15 minutes ❧ Cooking Time: 20 minutes ❧ Setting: Sauté and Manual
Pressure: High ❧ Release: Manual

1 tablespoon olive oil

½ cup chopped onion

½ cup chopped carrots

½ cup chopped celery

1 cup raw, pearl barley

1 teaspoon curry powder

A few golden raisins, *optional*

2½ cups low-sodium chicken stock or vegetable stock

1 tablespoon toasted sliced almonds

1 tablespoon snipped fresh parsley

TIP
You may replace the olive oil with canola or grapeseed oil if you wish.

1. Set the Instant Pot to Sauté and heat the oil in the inner pot.

2. Sauté the onion for 3 minutes. Add the carrots and celery and sauté for an additional 5 to 8 minutes. Press Cancel.

3. Add the barley, curry powder, raisins (if using), and stock.

4. Secure the lid and set the vent to sealing.

5. Manually set the cook time for 20 minutes on high pressure.

6. When the cooking time is over, manually release the pressure.

7. Stir in the almonds and parsley just before serving.

Non-Pantry-Staple Grocery List
- ½ cup chopped carrots
- ½ cup chopped celery
- 1 cup pearl barley
- A few golden raisins, *optional*
- 1 tablespoon toasted sliced almonds
- 1 tablespoon snipped fresh parsley

Calories 182

Fat 5 g

Fiber 6 g

Carbs 29 g

Net carbs 23 g

Sodium 165 mg

Sugar 3 g

Protein 7 g

Millet Casserole

Lizzie Ann Yoder, Hartville, OH

Makes 12 servings
Prep. Time: 8 minutes   ♣   Cooking Time: Manual   ♣   Setting: Manual
Pressure: High   ♣   Release: Natural then Manual

3 fresh tomatoes, roughly chopped

¾ cup salsa of your choice

2 garlic cloves

1 green bell pepper, cut up

1 cup millet

1¾ cups low-sodium vegetable stock or water

1. Place the tomatoes, salsa, garlic, and green pepper in a food processor and process for 20 to 30 seconds. Pour into the inner pot of the Instant Pot.

2. Pour the millet and stock into the inner pot.

3. Secure the lid and set the vent to sealing.

4. Manually set the cook time for 10 minutes.

5. When the cooking time is over, let the pressure release naturally for 10 minutes, then manually release the remaining pressure.

6. When the pin drops, remove the lid, stir, and enjoy!

Non-Pantry-Staple Grocery List
- 3 tomatoes
- ¾ cup salsa of your choice
- 1 green bell pepper
- 1 cup millet

Calories 75
Fat 1 g
Fiber 2 g
Carbs 15 g
Net carbs 13 g
Sodium 117 mg
Sugar 2 g
Protein 2 g

Golden Millet

Carolyn Spohn, Shawnee, KS

Makes 8 servings
Prep. Time: 10 minutes ⚜ Cooking Time: 10 minutes ⚜ Setting: Sauté and Manual
Pressure: High ⚜ Release: Natural then Manual

1 tablespoon extra-virgin olive oil
1 small onion, finely minced
1 garlic clove, minced
1 cup hulled, raw millet
4 medium carrots, peeled and shredded
1 1/4 cup low-fat low-sodium chicken stock
1/2 cup skim milk
1/4 teaspoon black pepper

TIP
You may replace the olive oil with canola or grapeseed oil if you wish.

Non-Pantry-Staple Grocery List
- 1 cup raw millet
- 4 medium carrots

---

1. Set the Instant Pot to Sauté and heat the oil in the inner pot.

2. Add the minced onion and cook for about 3 minutes until soft.

3. Add minced garlic and cook about 2 more minutes.

4. Push the onions and garlic to the outer edges of the inner pot and add the millet. Stir for a few minutes to lightly toast. Press Cancel.

5. Add the shredded carrots, chicken stock, milk, and pepper.

6. Secure the lid and set the vent to sealing.

7. Manually set the cook time for 10 minutes on high pressure.

8. When the cooking time is over, let the pressure release naturally for 10 minutes, then manually release the remaining pressure.

9. When the pin drops, open the lid, stir and serve.

Calories 145
Fat 3 g
Fiber 3 g
Carbs 24 g
Net carbs 21 g
Sodium 83 mg
Sugar 3 g
Protein 5 g

Desserts

Tasty Tofu Brownie Snacks

Mary Ann Lefever, Lancaster, PA

Makes 14 brownie snacks
Prep. Time: 15 minutes   ⚜   Cooking Time: 15 minutes   ⚜   Setting: Manual
Pressure: High   ⚜   Release: Natural then Manual   ⚜   Cooling Time: 15 minutes

Nonstick cooking spray

½ cup plus 2 tablespoons whole wheat pastry flour

¼ teaspoon baking soda

¼ teaspoon cinnamon

2 tablespoons plus 2 teaspoons cocoa powder, unsweetened

2 tablespoons unsweetened applesauce

½ teaspoon canola oil

¼ cup honey

½ package Mori-Nu Silken Lite Firm Tofu, drained

½ teaspoon vanilla extract

1 tablespoon chopped walnuts, *optional*

1 cup water

1. Spray 2 silicone egg bite molds with nonstick cooking spray.

2. In a food processor fitted with the metal chopping blade, process all the dry ingredients (excluding walnuts). Empty into small bowl and set aside.

3. Place all the wet ingredients in the food processor and process until smooth, scraping bowl sides occasionally.

4. Add dry mixture all at once to wet ingredients in food-processor bowl.

5. Pulse to blend until dry ingredients are just moistened.

6. Cover each egg bite mold with a piece of paper towel and foil secured over the top.

7. Divide the batter evenly between the egg bite molds. Sprinkle with nuts, if using.

Non-Pantry-Staple Grocery List
- ½ cup plus 2 tablespoons whole wheat pastry flour
- 2 tablespoons plus 2 teaspoons cocoa powder
- 2 tablespoons unsweetened applesauce
- ½ package Mori-Nu Silken Lite Firm Tofu
- 1 tablespoon chopped walnuts, *optional*

Calories 187
Fat 1 g
Fiber 1 g
Carbs 9 g
Net carbs 8 g
Sodium 24 mg
Sugar 5 g
Protein 1 g

TIP
You may exchange the canola oil with coconut oil if you wish.

8. Pour the water into the inner pot of the Instant Pot and place the trivet on top. Stack the covered silicone molds on top of the trivet.

9. Secure the lid and set the vent to sealing.

10. Manually set the cook time for 15 minutes on high pressure.

11. When the cooking time is over, let the pressure release naturally for 10 minutes, then manually release the remaining pressure.

12. Carefully remove the trivet with oven mitts and remove the foil and paper towel from the silicone molds. Let them cool on a cooling rack for 15 minutes. Then, pop the brownies out and enjoy!

Chocolate Bundt Cake

Margaret Wenger Johnson, Keezletown, VA

Makes 10 servings
Prep. Time: 15 minutes ❧ Cooking Time: 30 minutes ❧ Setting: Manual
Pressure: High ❧ Release: Natural ❧ Cooling Time: 20 minutes

1½ cups whole wheat pastry flour

½ cup turbinado sugar, or sugar of your choice

1½ tablespoons unsweetened cocoa powder

¼ teaspoon salt

1⅛ teaspoons baking soda

½ tablespoon vanilla extract

1 tablespoon white vinegar

¼ cup canola oil

1 cup boiling water

1 cup room-temperature water

Non-Pantry-Staple Grocery List
- 1½ cups whole wheat pastry flour
- 1½ tablespoons unsweetened cocoa powder
- 1 tablespoon white vinegar

Calories 148
Fat 6 g
Fiber 2 g
Carbs 23 g
Net carbs 21 g
Sodium 190 mg
Sugar 10 g
Protein 3 g

TIP
You may exchange the canola oil with coconut oil if you wish.

1. In a mixing bowl, sift together the flour, sugar, cocoa powder, salt, and baking soda.

2. Make 3 holes in the dry ingredients. Pour the vanilla, vinegar, and oil into those holes.

3. Add the boiling water. Beat for 2 minutes by hand, or with a mixer. (This will make a thin batter.)

4. Pour the batter into a greased 7-inch nonstick Bundt pan. Cover with foil.

5. Pour the room-temperature water into the inner pot of the Instant Pot and place the trivet on top.

6. Place the covered Bundt pan on top of the trivet in the inner pot. Secure the lid and set the vent to sealing.

7. Manually set the cook time for 30 minutes on high pressure.

8. When the cooking time is over, let the pressure release naturally.

9. When the pin drops, remove the lid and carefully remove the trivet with oven mitts.

10. Remove the foil and let the cake cool for about 20 minutes.

Ginger Crumb Cake

Mary Kathryn Yoder, Harrisonville, MO

Makes 9 servings
Prep. Time: 15 minutes ⚬ Cooking Time: 25 minutes ⚬ Setting: Manual
Pressure: High ⚬ Release: Natural then Manual

2 cups whole wheat flour

⅓ cup trans-fat-free buttery spread

I cup turbinado sugar, or sugar of your choice

¼ teaspoon baking soda

I teaspoon baking powder

½ teaspoon nutmeg

½ teaspoon ground ginger

½ teaspoon cinnamon

Egg substitute equivalent to I egg, or 2 egg whites

½ cup low-fat buttermilk

I cup water

Non-Pantry-Staple Grocery List
• 2 cups whole wheat flour
• ½ cup low-fat buttermilk

Calories 211

Fat 8 g

Fiber 3 g

Carbs 32 g

Net carbs 29 g

Sodium 115 mg

Sugar 13 g

Protein 5 g

1. In a large bowl, mix the flour and buttery spread with a pastry cutter until crumbs the size of peas form.

2. Add sugar. Mix with your hands to blend thoroughly.

3. Measure out ⅞ cup crumbs. Set aside for topping.

4. Measure out another ⅞ cup crumbs. Spread in the bottom of a greased 7-inch nonstick Bundt pan.

5. To the remaining 1¾ cups crumbs in mixing bowl, add the baking soda, baking powder, and spices.

6. When thoroughly blended, beat in the egg substitute and buttermilk.

7. Spoon the batter into the Bundt pan, being careful not to disturb crumbs on bottom of pan.

8. Top the batter with the reserved ⅞ cup crumbs.

9. Pour the water into the inner pot of the Instant Pot. Place the trivet on top.

10. Place the Bundt pan on top of the trivet in the inner pot. Secure the lid and set the vent to sealing.

11. Manually set the time to cook for 25 minutes on high pressure.

12. When the cooking time is over, let the pressure release naturally for 10 minutes, then manually release the remaining pressure.

13. When the pin drops, remove the lid and test the doneness by inserting a toothpick into the center. If it comes out clean, it's done! If it needs more time, reseal the lid and set the vent back to sealing and cook an additional 2 minutes.

Strawberry Shortcake

Joanna Harrison, Lafayette, CO

Makes 8 servings

Prep. Time: 25 minutes & Cooking Time: 40 minutes

Setting: Manual & Pressure: High & Release: Natural then Manual & Cooling Time: 7 minutes

1 quart (4 cups) fresh strawberries

3 tablespoons agave nectar, or honey, *divided*

1½ cups whole wheat pastry flour

1 teaspoon baking powder

⅛ teaspoon salt

¼ cup trans-fat-free buttery spread

Egg substitute equivalent to 1 egg, or 2 egg whites

½ cup skim milk

1 cup water

Non-Pantry-Staple Grocery List

- 1 qt. strawberries
- 1½ cups whole wheat pastry flour
- 3 tablespoons agave nectar or honey

Calories 182

Fat 7 g

Fiber 4 g

Carbs 29 g

Net carbs 25 g

Sodium 97 mg

Sugar 10 g

Protein 5 g

1. Mash or slice the strawberries in a bowl. Stir in 2 tablespoons agave nectar. Set aside and refrigerate.

2. In a large mixing bowl, combine the flour, baking powder, salt, and 1 tablespoon agave nectar.

3. Cut the buttery spread into the dry ingredients with a pastry cutter or 2 knives until crumbly.

4. In a small bowl, beat the egg substitute and milk together.

5. Stir the wet ingredients into the flour mixture just until moistened.

6. Pour the batter into a greased 7-inch Bundt pan. Cover tightly with foil.

7. Pour the water into the inner pot and place the trivet on top. Place the Bundt pan on top of the trivet in the inner pot. Secure the lid and set the vent to sealing.

8. Manually set the cook time for 40 minutes on high pressure.

9. When cooking time is up, allow the pressure to release naturally for 10 minutes, then manually release the remaining pressure.

10. When the pin drops, remove the lid and carefully lift the trivet out of the inner pot with oven mitts.

11. Allow cake to cool to cool in the pan for 7 minutes, then remove onto the cooling rack.

12. Cut the cake into desired servings and spoon berries over the top.

Dessert Filled Apples

Jean Butzer, Batavia, NY

Makes 4 servings
Prep. Time: 10 minutes ⚬ Baking Time: 30–40 minutes

4 medium tart apples, cored, but left whole and unpeeled

Nonstick cooking spray

4 teaspoons no-sugar-added strawberry jam

½ teaspoon ground cinnamon

1½ cups orange juice

1 cup water

Serving Suggestion:

Top with a bit of your favorite healthy granola for an added crunch.

1. Place the apples in a foil-lined 7-inch round baking pan, generously greased with nonstick cooking spray.

2. Spoon 1 teaspoon jam into the center of each apple.

3. Sprinkle each apple with cinnamon.

4. Pour the orange juice into the pan around the apples.

5. Pour the water into the inner pot of the Instant Pot. Place the trivet on top.

6. Place the 7-inch round baking pan on top of the trivet in the inner pot.

7. Secure the lid and set the vent to sealing.

8. Manually set the cook time for 7 minutes on high pressure.

9. When the cooking time is over, let the pressure release naturally for 5 minutes, then release the remaining pressure manually.

Non-Pantry-Staple Grocery List
- 4 medium tart apples
- 4 teaspoons no-sugar-added strawberry fruit spread
- 1½ cups orange juice

Calories 173

Fat 0.5 g

Fiber 5 g

Carbs 44 g

Net carbs 39 g

Sodium 4 mg

Sugar 39 g

Protein 1 g

Keto-Style Crème Brûlée

Hope Comerford, Clinton Township, MI

Makes 4–6 servings
Prep. Time: 25 minutes   ✿   Cooking Time: 13 minutes   ✿   Setting: Manual   ✿   Pressure: Low
Release: Natural then Manual   ✿   Refrigeration Time: 4 hours   ✿   Broil Time: 3–10 minutes

5 egg yolks

2 cups heavy cream

¼ cup granulated erythritol

1 tablespoon high-quality vanilla extract

Pinch salt

1 cup water

2 tablespoons powdered erythritol

Fresh berries, to garnish, *optional*

1. In a medium mixing bowl, beat the egg yolks.

2. Slowly pour in the cream and the granulated erythritol while mixing. Add the vanilla and salt.

3. Pour the mixture evenly into 6 6-inch ramekins. You can use a spoon to pop any air bubbles on top. Cover each ramekin tightly with foil.

4. Pour the water into the inner pot of the Instant Pot and place the trivet on top. Carefully arrange your ramekins in 2 layers, staggering the top layer on top of the bottom layer.

5. Secure the lid and set the vent to sealing.

6. Manually set the time to cook for 13 minutes on low pressure.

7. When the cooking time is over, let the pressure release naturally for 15 minutes, then release the remaining pressure.

Non-Pantry-Staple Grocery List
- 2 cups heavy cream
- ¼ cup granulated erythritol
- 2 tablespoons powdered erythritol
- Fresh berries for garnish, *optional*

Calories 323
Fat 33 g
Fiber 0 g
Carbs 14 g
Net carbs 14 g
Sodium 28 mg
Sugar 3 g
Protein 4.5 g

8. When the pin drops, remove the lid and check for doneness. If the center is jiggly, you're in good shape. If the whole thing is jiggly, re-cover, replace the lid, set the vent back to sealing and cook on low pressure an additional 3 minutes.

9. Refrigerate the ramekins for 2 hours.

10. Sprinkle the powdered erythritol evenly over the top. Broil for 3 to 10 minutes, until the sugar is bubbly and browning. Watch carefully! Or if you own a kitchen torch, use that instead to caramelize the sugar.

11. Return the crème brûlée to the refrigerator for at least 2 more hours. Serve cold with a few beautiful berries to garnish.

Chunky Applesauce

Hope Comerford, Clinton Township, MI

Makes 10 servings
Prep. Time: 10 minutes ☙ Cooking Time: 5 minutes
Setting: Manual ☙ Pressure: High ☙ Release: Natural then Manual

3 lb. tart apples, peeled, cored, sliced

⅓ cup honey

¾ cup water

1 teaspoon lemon zest

3 tablespoons lemon juice

3 cinnamon sticks

1. Place all ingredients in the Instant Pot. Stir to coat all the apples.

2. Secure the lid and set the vent to sealing.

3. Manually set the cook time for 5 minutes on high pressure.

4. When the cooking time is over, let the pressure release naturally for 10 minutes, then manually release the remaining pressure.

5. When the pin drops, remove the lid. Remove the cinnamon sticks and mash the applesauce mixture lightly with a potato masher.

Non-Pantry-Staple Grocery List
- 3 lb. tart apples
- 1 lemon (for juice and zest)
- 3 cinnamon sticks

Calories 107
Fat 0 g
Fiber 4 g
Carbs 29 g
Net carbs 25 g
Sodium 3 mg
Sugar 23 g
Protein 0.5 g

Coconut Rice Pudding

Hope Comerford, Clinton Township, MI

Makes 6 servings
Prep. Time: 2 minutes 🍃 Cooking Time: 10 minutes 🍃 Setting: Porridge 🍃 Release: Natural

1 cup arborio rice, rinsed

1 cup unsweetened almond milk

14-ounce can light coconut milk

½ cup water

½ cup turbinado sugar, or sugar of your choice

1 stick cinnamon

¼ cup dried cranberries, *optional*

¼ cup unsweetened coconut flakes, *optional*

1. Place the rice into the inner pot of the Instant Pot, along with all of the remaining ingredients (except optional ingredients).

2. Secure the lid and set the vent to sealing.

3. Using the Porridge setting, set the cook time for 10 minutes.

4. When the cooking time is over, let the pressure release naturally.

5. When the pin drops, remove the lid and remove cinnamon stick.

6. Stir and serve as is or sprinkle some cranberries and unsweetened coconut flakes on top of each serving. Enjoy!

Non-Pantry-Staple Grocery List
- 1 cup arborio rice
- 1 stick cinnamon
- 1 cup dried cranberries, *optional*
- ¼ cup unsweetened coconut flakes, *optional*

Calories 354
Fat 6 g
Fiber 3 g
Carbs 74 g
Net carbs 71 g
Sodium 87 mg
Sugar 43 g
Protein 4 g

Rice Pudding

Betty Moore, Plano, IL

Makes 6 servings
Prep. Time: 8 minutes   Cooking Time: 25 minutes   Setting: Manual
Pressure: High   Release: Natural

1 cup brown rice
½ cup raisins
1 egg
3 egg whites
16 ounces fat-free evaporated milk
1 cup water
⅓ cup brown sugar
1 teaspoon vanilla extract
⅛ teaspoon nutmeg, *optional*

1. Pour the rice into the inner pot of the Instant Pot. Sprinkle the raisins over the top.

2. In a medium bowl, combine the egg, egg whites, milk, water, sugar, vanilla, and nutmeg (if using). Mix well. Pour this over the rice and raisins.

3. Secure the lid and set the vent to sealing.

4. Manually set the cook time for 25 minutes on high pressure.

5. When the cooking time is over, let the pressure release naturally.

6. When the pin drops, remove the lid and stir.

7. Serve immediately, or warm gently before serving.

Non-Pantry-Staple Grocery List
- ½ cup raisins
- 16 ounces fat-free evaporated milk

Calories 303
Fat 8 g
Fiber 2 g
Carbs 49 g
Net carbs 47 g
Sodium 126 mg
Sugar 23 g
Protein 11 g

Tapioca Pudding

Nancy W. Huber, Green Park, PA

Makes 12 servings
Prep. Time: 5 minutes ❧ Cooking Time: 15 minutes ❧ Setting: Manual then Sauté
Pressure: High ❧ Release: Natural then Manual

3 cups fat-free milk
1 cup water
1 cup small pearl tapioca
½ cup honey
4 eggs, beaten
1 teaspoon vanilla extract

1. Combine the milk, water, tapioca, and honey in the inner pot of the Instant Pot.

2. Secure the lid and set the vent to sealing.

3. Manually set the cook time for 6 minutes on high pressure.

4. When the cooking time is over, let the pressure release naturally for 10 minutes, then release any remaining pressure manually.

5. When the pin drops, remove the lid. Press Cancel.

6. Press the Sauté button.

7. In a bowl, mix the eggs and vanilla. Remove about ½ cup of the pudding from the inner pot and mix vigorously with the egg/vanilla mixture to temper the eggs. Then, add this mixture back to the rest of the pudding slowly, stirring. When it comes to a boil, press Cancel and remove the inner pot from the Instant Pot.

8. Let the pudding cool down to room temperature, then chill it for at least 4 hours.

Non-Pantry-Staple Grocery List
• 1 cup small pearl tapioca

Calories 134
Fat 2 g
Fiber 0 g
Carbs 23 g
Net carbs 23 g
Sodium 5 mg
Sugar 15 g
Protein 4 g

snacks

Insta Popcorn

Hope Comerford, Clinton Township, MI

Makes 5–6 servings
Prep. Time: 1 minute ♣ *Cooking Time: about 5 minutes* ♣ *Setting: Sauté*

2 tablespoons coconut oil

½ cup popcorn kernels

¼ cup margarine spread, melted, *optional*

Sea salt to taste

1. Set the Instant Pot to Sauté.

2. Melt the coconut oil in the inner pot, then add the popcorn kernels and stir.

3. Press Adjust to bring the temperature up to high.

4. When the corn starts popping, secure the lid on the Instant Pot.

5. When you no longer hear popping, turn off the Instant Pot, remove the lid, and carefully pour the popcorn into a bowl.

6. Top with the optional melted margarine and season the popcorn with sea salt to your liking.

Non-Pantry-Staple Grocery List
- ½ cup popcorn kernels

Calories 161
Fat 13 g
Fiber 3 g
Carbs 13 g
Net carbs 10 g
Sodium 89 mg
Sugar 0 g
Protein 2 g

Hope's Family Hummus

Hope Comerford, Clinton Township, MI

Makes 24 servings; about 2 tablespoons/serving
Soaking Time: 8 hours, or overnight ❧ Prep. Time: 15 minutes ❧ Cooking Time: 25 minutes
Setting: Manual ❧ Pressure: High ❧ Release: Natural

16-ounce bag dried garbanzo beans, soaked overnight

12 cups water

3 tablespoons tahini

$\frac{1}{4}$–$\frac{1}{2}$ cup lemon juice (depending on your taste)

1 garlic clove

$\frac{1}{8}$ teaspoon cumin

$\frac{1}{8}$ teaspoon salt

$\frac{1}{4}$ cup extra-virgin olive oil, *optional*

Non-Pantry-Staple Grocery List
- 16-ounce bag dried garbanzo beans
- 3 tablespoons tahini
- $\frac{1}{4}$–$\frac{1}{2}$ cup lemon juice

TIP
If you do not have time, don't want to, or forget to soak the garbanzo beans, increase the cook time by 10 minutes.

1. Place the garbanzo beans into the inner pot of the Instant Pot. Pour in the water.

2. Secure the lid and set the vent to sealing.

3. Manually set the cook time to 25 minutes on high pressure.

4. When the cooking time is over, let the pressure release naturally. This will take around a half hour.

5. Drain off any liquid. Pour the beans into a food processor.

6. When the pin drops, remove the lid. Carefully remove the inner pot and drain the liquid from the beans.

7. Add the tahini, lemon juice, garlic, cumin, and salt into the beans in the food processor and add water so that it reaches just below the level of the beans. Note: If you're unsure of how much lemon juice you want to add, start with less, taste, and add more if you desire. Blend until smooth.

8. Place the hummus in a serving dish. Drizzle with the olive oil if you choose.

Calories 83
Fat 2 g
Fiber 2 g
Carbs 13 g
Net carbs 11 g
Sodium 19 mg
Sugar 2 g
Protein 4 g

Serving Suggestion:
My favorite way to serve this is with fresh carrot slices!

Spinach and Artichoke Dip

Michele Ruvola, Vestal, NY

Makes 10–12 servings
Prep. Time: 5 minutes ⚹ Cooking Time: 4 minutes ⚹ Setting: Manual
Pressure: High ⚹ Release: Manual

8 ounces low-fat cream cheese
10-ounce box frozen spinach
½ cup no-sodium chicken broth
14-ounce can artichoke hearts, drained
½ cup low-fat sour cream
½ cup low-fat mayonnaise
3 garlic cloves, minced
1 teaspoon onion powder
16 ounces shredded reduced-fat
Parmesan cheese

TIP
This dip will
thicken as it cools.

1. Put all ingredients in the inner pot of the Instant Pot, except the Parmesan cheese.

2. Secure the lid and set the vent to sealing. Manually set for 4 minutes on high pressure.

3. Manually release the pressure when the cooking time is over.

4. When the pin drops, open the lid and immediately stir in the cheese.

Serving Suggestion:
Serve with vegetables or sliced whole-grain bread.

Non-Pantry-Staple Grocery List
- 8 ounces low-fat cream cheese
- 10 ounces frozen spinach
- 14-ounce can artichoke hearts
- ½ cup low-fat sour cream
- ½ cup low-fat mayonnaise
- 1 teaspoon onion powder
- 16 ounces shredded reduced-fat Parmesan cheese

Calories 244
Fat 15 g
Fiber 3 g
Carbs 15 g
Net carbs 12 g
Sodium 900 mg
Sugar 3 g
Protein 15 g

Smoky Barbecue Meatballs

Carla Koslowsky, Hillsboro, KS
Sherry Kreider, Lancaster, PA
Jennie Martin, Richfield, PA

Makes 10 servings, 1 meatball per serving
Prep. Time: 10 minutes   ☙   Cook Time: 19 minutes   ☙   Setting: Sauté then Manual
Pressure: High   ☙   Release: Manual

1½ pounds 90% lean ground beef

½ cup quick oats

½ cup fat-free evaporated milk, or milk

¼ cup egg substitute

¼–½ cup finely chopped onion, *optional*

¼ teaspoon garlic powder

¼ teaspoon pepper

¼ teaspoon chili powder

1 teaspoon salt

2 tablespoons olive oil

Sauce:

1½ cups reduced-sugar ketchup

½ cup water

6 tablespoons Splenda Brown Sugar Blend

¼ cup chopped onion

¼ teaspoon liquid smoke

1. Mix the ground beef, oats, milk, egg substitute, onion, garlic powder, pepper, chili powder, and salt. Form 10 balls, each weighing about 2 ounces.

2. Set the Instant Pot to Sauté and pour the olive oil into the inner pot. Once warm, add the meatballs one at a time. Just try to make sure they're lightly browned on at least two sides. Turn the Instant Pot off by pressing Cancel.

3. Remove the meatballs onto a paper-towel-lined plate and wipe the inner pot mostly clean of bits of meat and oil. Put the meatballs back into the inner pot.

4. Mix the sauce ingredients in a small bowl, then pour them over the meatballs.

5. Secure the lid and make sure the vent is set to sealing. Cook on the Manual setting for 4 minutes.

6. When the cooking time is over, manually release the pressure.

7. When the pin drops, remove the lid and press cancel. Press Sauté and allow the sauce to simmer until it is thickened to your liking.

Non-Pantry-Staple Grocery List
- 1½ lb. 90% lean ground beef
- ½ cup quick oats
- ½ cup fat-free evaporated milk, or milk
- 1½ cups reduced-sugar ketchup
- 6 tablespoons Splenda Brown Sugar Blend
- ¼ teaspoon liquid smoke

TIP
You may replace the olive oil with canola or grapeseed oil if you wish.

Calories 247

Fat 10 g

Fiber 1 g

Carbs 22 g

Net carbs 21 g

Sodium 448 mg

Sugar 17 g

Protein 16 g

Breads/Muffins

Sour Cream Corn Bread

Edwina Stoltzfus, Narvon, PA

Makes 9 servings
Prep. Time: 10 minutes ⚜ Cooking Time: 55 minutes ⚜ Setting: Manual
Pressure: High ⚜ Release: Natural then Manual

Egg substitute equivalent to 1 egg, or 2 egg whites, beaten

¼ cup skim milk

2 tablespoons canola oil

1 cup fat-free sour cream

¾ cup cornmeal

½ cup whole wheat flour

½ cup all-purpose flour

¼ cup turbinado sugar, or sugar of your choice

2 teaspoons baking powder

½ teaspoon baking soda

Nonstick cooking spray

1 cup water

TIP

You may replace the canola oil with coconut oil if you prefer.

1. In a large mixing bowl, beat the egg substitute.

2. Add the milk, oil, and sour cream and combine well.

3. In a separate bowl, combine all dry ingredients.

4. Add the dry ingredients to the wet ingredients. Mix just until moistened.

5. Spoon into a 7- by 3-inch round baking pan, sprayed lightly with nonstick cooking spray. Wrap the top tightly with foil, then take a second piece of foil and wrap the bottom too.

6. Pour the water into the inner pot of the Instant Pot. Place the trivet on top.

7. Place the foil-wrapped baking pan on the trivet. Secure the lid and set the vent to sealing.

8. Manually set the time to cook for 55 minutes on high pressure.

Non-Pantry-Staple Grocery List
- 1 cup fat-free sour cream
- ¾ cup cornmeal
- ½ cup whole wheat flour
- ½ cup all-purpose flour
- 2 teaspoons baking soda
- ½ teaspoon baking powder

Calories 159

Fat 3 g

Fiber 1 g

Carbs 27 g

Net carbs 26 g

Sodium 293 mg

Sugar 5 g

Protein 4 g

9. When the cooking time is over, let the pressure release naturally for 10 minutes, then manually release the remaining pressure.

10. Carefully remove the trivet with oven mitts. Wipe any moisture off of the foil, then carefully remove the foil from the pan.

11. Serve warm!

Serving Suggestion:
Serve with Chicken Chili Pepper Stew from page 68.

Apple Cranberry Muffin Bites

Hope Comerford, Clinton Township, MI

Makes 14 muffin bites
Prep. Time: 10 minutes & Cooking Time: 13 minutes & Setting: Manual
Pressure: High & Release: Natural then Manual

1⅓ cups whole wheat flour

⅓ cup brown sugar

2 teaspoons baking powder

½ teaspoon baking soda

½ teaspoon cinnamon

2 eggs, or 4 egg whites

¼ cup unsweetened applesauce

1 teaspoon orange zest

1 tablespoon freshly squeezed orange juice

1 cup nonfat plain Greek yogurt

1 large Granny Smith apple, peeled and shredded

½ cup fresh, or frozen and unthawed, cranberries cut in half

Nonstick cooking spray

1 cup water

1. In a bowl, mix the whole wheat flour, brown sugar, baking powder, baking soda, and cinnamon.

2. In a separate bowl, mix the eggs, applesauce, orange zest, orange juice, and Greek yogurt.

3. Gently fold in the shredded apple and cranberries.

4. Spray 2 silicone egg bite molds with nonstick cooking spray.

5. Fill each mold ¾ of the way full of batter. Cover the molds with foil.

6. Pour the water into the inner pot of the Instant Pot.

7. Stack both filled silicone molds onto the trivet and carefully lower the trivet into the inner pot.

8. Secure the lid and set the vent to sealing.

continued

Non-Pantry-Staple Grocery List
- 1⅓ cups whole wheat flour
- ¼ cup unsweetened applesauce
- 1 orange (for zest and juice)
- 1 cup nonfat plain Greek yogurt
- 1 large Granny Smith apple
- ½ cup fresh or frozen cranberries

Calories 81

Fat 1 g

Fiber 1 g

Carbs 15 g

Net carbs 14 g

Sodium 114 mg

Sugar 6 g

Protein 4 g

9. Manually select 13 minutes of cooking time on high pressure.

10. When the cooking time is over, let the pressure release naturally for 10 minutes, then manually release the remaining pressure.

11. Remove the lid and carefully lift the trivet and molds out of the pot with oven mitts.

12. Remove the foil and allow the muffins to cool. Pop them out of the molds onto a plate or serving platter.

Banana Bread Bites

Hope Comerford, Clinton Township, MI

Makes 14 banana bread bites
Prep. Time: 10 minutes ❧ Cooking Time: 10 minutes ❧ Setting: Manual
Pressure: High ❧ Release: Natural then Manual

1½ cups gluten-free cup-for-cup flour
½ cup gluten-free old-fashioned oats
1 teaspoon baking soda
½ teaspoon cinnamon
¼ teaspoon nutmeg
¼ teaspoon salt
3 very ripe bananas, mashed
⅓ cup unsweetened applesauce
½ cup honey
2 eggs
1 teaspoon vanilla extract
Nonstick cooking spray
1 cup water

Non-Pantry-Staple Grocery List
- 1½ cups gluten-free cup-for-cup flour
- ½ cup gluten-free old-fashioned oats
- 3 very ripe bananas
- ⅓ cup unsweetened applesauce

Calories 129
Fat 1 g
Fiber 2 g
Carbs 28 g
Net carbs 26 g
Sodium 135 mg
Sugar 14 g
Protein 3 g

1. In a bowl, mix the flour, oats, baking soda, cinnamon, nutmeg, and salt.

2. In a separate bowl, mix the mashed bananas, applesauce, honey, eggs, and vanilla.

3. Mix the wet ingredients into the dry ingredients, only until just combined. Do not overmix.

4. Spray 2 silicone egg bite molds with nonstick cooking spray.

5. Fill each mold ¾ of the way full of batter. Cover the molds with foil.

6. Pour the water into the inner pot of the Instant Pot.

7. Stack both filled silicone molds onto the trivet and carefully lower the trivet into the inner pot.

8. Secure the lid and set the vent to sealing.

9. Manually select 10 minutes of cooking time on high pressure.

10. When the cooking time is over, let the pressure release naturally for 5 minutes, then manually release the remaining pressure.

11. Remove the lid and carefully lift the trivet and molds out of the pot with oven mitts.

12. Remove the foil and allow the banana bread bites to cool. Pop them out of the molds onto a plate or serving platter.

Metric Equivalent Measurements

If you're accustomed to using metric measurements, I don't want you to be inconvenienced by the imperial measurements I use in this book.

Weight (Dry Ingredients)

1 oz		30 g
4 oz	¼ lb	120 g
8 oz	½ lb	240 g
12 oz	¾ lb	360 g
16 oz	1 lb	480 g
32 oz	2 lb	960 g

Volume (Liquid Ingredients)

½ tsp.		2 ml
1 tsp.		5 ml
1 Tbsp.	½ fl oz	15 ml
2 Tbsp.	1 fl oz	30 ml
¼ cup	2 fl oz	60 ml
⅓ cup	3 fl oz	80 ml
½ cup	4 fl oz	120 ml
⅔ cup	5 fl oz	160 ml
¾ cup	6 fl oz	180 ml
1 cup	8 fl oz	240 ml
1 pt	16 fl oz	480 ml
1 qt	32 fl oz	960 ml

Length

¼ in	6 mm
½ in	13 mm
¾ in	19 mm
1 in	25 mm
6 in	15 cm
12 in	30 cm

Recipe and Ingredient Index

A

allspice
Curried Carrot Bisque, 53
almonds
Curried Barley, 165
Lemon Curry Rice Mix, 159
Spiced Lentils with Chicken and Rice, 121
Apple Cranberry Muffin Bites, 197–198
Apple-Cranberry Wild Rice, 161
apple juice
Braised Beef with Cranberries, 105
Squash Apple Bake, 143
apples
Breakfast Apples, 27
Dessert Filled Apples, 177
dried
Apple-Cranberry Wild Rice, 161
Squash Apple Bake, 143
applesauce
Apple Cranberry Muffin Bites, 197–198
Banana Bread Bites, 199
Chunky Applesauce, 180
Giant Healthy Pancake, 12
Tasty Tofu Brownie Snacks, 170–171
artichoke hearts
Spinach and Artichoke Dip, 189
Artichokes and Brown Rice, 160
asparagus
Creamy Asparagus Soup, 50

B

bacon
Delectable Eggplant, 83–84
Easy Quiche, 26
Baked Eggs, 21
Banana Bread Bites, 199
Barbacoa Beef, 103
Barbecue Lentils, 163
barley
Beef Mushroom Barley Soup, 72
Chicken Barley Soup, 65
Curried Barley, 165
Hearty Vegetable Soup, 69
Lentil and Barley Soup, 38
Lentil Barley Stew with Chicken, 61
Scrumptious Breakfast Barley, 16

Barley Risotto with Grilled Peppers, 97
basil
Cannellini Bean Soup, 34
Chicken Dinner in a Packet, 115
Chicken Noodle Soup, 63
Delectable Eggplant, 83–84
Eggplant Parmesan Lightened Up, 85
Flavorful Tomato Soup, 49
Garden Vegetable Soup with Pasta, 54
Hearty Vegetable Soup, 69
Herbed Fish Fillets, 129
Pasta Primavera, 101
Spinach and Mushroom Frittata, 29
Tomato and Barley Soup, 41
Turkey Sausage and Cabbage Soup, 62
beans
black
Black Bean Soup with Fresh Salsa, 35
cannellini
Cannellini Bean Soup, 34
Sausage, Beans, and Rice Soup, 59
Senate Bean Soup, 77
garbanzo
Chicken Casablanca, 122
Hope's Family Hummus, 188
Moroccan Spiced Sweet Potato Medley, 86
green
Napa Cabbage and Pork Soup, 80
kidney
Veggie Minestrone, 57
navy
Ham and Bean Soup, 75
white
White Bean Soup, 33
beef
ground
Beef and Black Bean Chili, 73
Beef and Zucchini Casserole, 107
Hearty Vegetable Soup, 69
Smoky Barbecue Meatballs, 191
Stuffed Cabbage, 109–109
Stuffed Sweet Pepper Soup, 71
Tomato Beef Soup, 74
round roast
Mexican-Inspired Bottom Round Roast, 106
Beef and Black Bean Chili, 73

Beef and Zucchini Casserole, 107
Beef Mushroom Barley Soup, 72
beets
    Seasoned Beets, 144
bell pepper
    Barley Risotto with Grilled Peppers, 97
    Broccoli and Bell Peppers, 149
    Delectable Eggplant, 83–84
    Garden Vegetable Crustless Quiche, 87
    Garden Vegetable Soup with Pasta, 54
    Ham and Bean Soup, 75
    Healthy Joes, 114
    Hometown Spanish Rice, 157
    Lentils with Cheese, 102
    Millet Casserole, 167
    Moroccan Spiced Sweet Potato Medley, 86
    Paprika Pork Chops with Rice, 113
    Rosemary Carrots, 151
    Spicy Chicken Soup with Edamame, 67
    Stuffed Sweet Pepper Soup, 71
    Sweet Potato Soup with Roasted Red Peppers &
        Vegetables, 47
    To-Go Crustless Veggie Quiche Cups, 24–25
    Tomato Beef Soup, 74
    White Bean Soup, 33
    Zesty Pumpkin Soup, 55
Black Bean Soup with Fresh Salsa, 35
Braised Beef with Cranberries, 105
bread
    Banana Bread Bites, 199
    Cinnamon French Toast, 11
    Sour Cream Corn Bread, 194–195
bread crumbs
    Simple Salmon, 131
    Turkey Meat Loaf, 126–127
breakfast
    Baked Eggs, 21
    Cinnamon French Toast, 11
    Delicious Shirred Eggs, 23
    Easy Quiche, 26
    Giant Healthy Pancake, 12
    Grain and Fruit Breakfast, 17
    Instant Pot Yogurt, 30
    Insta-Oatmeal, 15
    Perfect Instant Pot Hard-Boiled Eggs, 19
    Poached Eggs, 20
    Pumpkin Spice Pancake Bites, 13
    Scrumptious Breakfast Barley, 16
    Spinach and Mushroom Frittata, 29
    To-Go Crustless Veggie Quiche Cups, 24–25

Breakfast Apples, 27
broccoli
    Italian Chicken and Broccoli, 125
    Lighter Cream of Broccoli Soup, 51
    To-Go Crustless Veggie Quiche Cups, 24–25
Broccoli and Bell Peppers, 149
broccolini
    Pasta Primavera, 101
Broccoli with Garlic, 148
Bulgur Pilaf, 164

C
cabbage
    Napa Cabbage and Pork Soup, 79
    Stuffed Cabbage, 109–109
    Turkey Sausage and Cabbage Soup, 62
Caesar dressing
    Caesar Salmon Fillets, 138
Caesar Salmon Fillets, 138
cake
    Chocolate Bundt Cake, 173
    Ginger Crumb Cake, 174
    Strawberry Shortcake, 175
Cannellini Bean Soup, 34
capers
    Wild Salmon with Capers, 134–135
cardamom
    Spiced Lentils with Chicken and Rice, 121
carrots
    Curried Carrot Bisque, 53
    Rosemary Carrots, 151
    Vegetable Medley, 153
casserole
    Beef and Zucchini Casserole, 107
    Millet Casserole, 167
Cauliflower Mashed Potatoes, 147
cheese
    cheddar
        Baked Eggs, 21
        Beef and Black Bean Chili, 73
        Cheesy Chicken and Rice, 120
        Easy Quiche, 26
        Lentils with Cheese, 102
        Lighter Cream of Broccoli Soup, 51
        To-Go Crustless Veggie Quiche Cups, 24–25
    cottage
        Baked Eggs, 21
        Garden Vegetable Crustless Quiche, 87
    cream
        Spinach and Artichoke Dip, 189

feta
    Greek-Style Halibut Steaks, 130
Garden Vegetable Crustless Quiche, 87
Gruyère
    Spinach and Mushroom Frittata, 29
Mediterranean Lentil Soup, 37
mozzarella
    Delectable Eggplant, 83–84
    Spinach Pie, 89
    Summer Squash Pie, 92
Parmesan
    Barley Risotto with Grilled Peppers, 97
    Beef and Zucchini Casserole, 107
    Cannellini Bean Soup, 34
    Delicious Shirred Eggs, 23
    Eggplant Parmesan Lightened Up, 85
    Hometown Spanish Rice, 157
    Italian Chicken and Broccoli, 125
    Mushroom Risotto, 95
    Pasta Primavera, 101
    Pumpkin Risotto, 96
    Spinach and Artichoke Dip, 189
    Spinach Pie, 89
    Turkey Peasant Soup, 60
    Veggie Minestrone, 57
Swiss
    Lentil and Barley Soup, 38
Cheesy Chicken and Rice, 120
chia seeds
    Breakfast Apples, 27
chicken
    Italian Chicken and Broccoli, 125
    Skinny Chicken Stroganoff, 117
    Spiced Lentils with Chicken and Rice, 121
Chicken Barley Soup, 65
Chicken Casablanca, 122
Chicken Chili Pepper Stew, 68
Chicken Dinner in a Packet, 115
Chicken Noodle Soup, 63
Chicken Rice Bake, 119
chili
    Beef and Black Bean Chili, 73
chipotle in adobo
    Barbacoa Beef, 103
chives
    Salmon with Chives, 133
Chocolate Bundt Cake, 173
Chunky Applesauce, 180
cilantro
    Black Bean Soup with Fresh Salsa, 35

Chicken Chili Pepper Stew, 68
Cilantro Lime Rice, 156
Curried Carrot Bisque, 53
Ham and Bean Soup, 75
Indian Tomato Rice Soup, 42
Moroccan Spiced Sweet Potato Medley, 86
Spiced Lentils with Chicken and Rice, 121
Cilantro Lime Rice, 156
cinnamon
    Apple Cranberry Muffin Bites, 197–198
    Banana Bread Bites, 199
    Chicken Casablanca, 122
    Chunky Applesauce, 180
    Coconut Rice Pudding, 181
    Dessert Filled Apples, 177
    Ginger Crumb Cake, 174
    Grain and Fruit Breakfast, 17
    Insta-Oatmeal, 15
    Pumpkin Spice Pancake Bites, 13
    Squash Apple Bake, 143
    Tasty Tofu Brownie Snacks, 170–171
Cinnamon French Toast, 11
cloves
    White Bean Soup, 33
cocoa powder
    Chocolate Bundt Cake, 173
    Tasty Tofu Brownie Snacks, 170–171
coconut
    Coconut Rice Pudding, 181
Coconut Rice Pudding, 181
cod
    Herbed Fish Fillets, 129
coriander
    Curried Carrot Bisque, 53
    Indian Tomato Rice Soup, 42
    Moroccan Spiced Sweet Potato Medley, 86
    Sweet Potato Soup with Kale, 46
    Zesty Pumpkin Soup, 55
corn
    Chicken Chili Pepper Stew, 68
cracker crumbs
    Summer Squash Pie, 92
cranberries
    Apple Cranberry Muffin Bites, 197–198
    Apple-Cranberry Wild Rice, 161
    Braised Beef with Cranberries, 105
    Coconut Rice Pudding, 181
    Grain and Fruit Breakfast, 17
    Scrumptious Breakfast Barley, 16
Creamy Asparagus Soup, 50

Recipe and Ingredient Index   203

Creamy Wild Rice Mushroom Soup, 43
crème brûlée
    Keto-Style Crème Brûlée, 178–179
cumin
    Barbacoa Beef, 103
    Black Bean Soup with Fresh Salsa, 35
    Chicken Casablanca, 122
    Chicken Chili Pepper Stew, 68
    Ham and Bean Soup, 75
    Hope's Family Hummus, 188
    Indian Tomato Rice Soup, 42
    Lemon Curry Rice Mix, 159
    Mexican-Inspired Bottom Round Roast, 106
    Moroccan Spiced Sweet Potato Medley, 86
    Spiced Lentils with Chicken and Rice, 121
Curried Barley, 165
Curried Carrot Bisque, 53
curry powder
    Curried Barley, 165
    Curried Carrot Bisque, 53
    Lemon Curry Rice Mix, 159

D
Delectable Eggplant, 83–84
Delicious Shirred Eggs, 23
Dessert Filled Apples, 177
dill
    Chicken Rice Bake, 119
    Herbed Fish Fillets, 129
    Napa Cabbage and Pork Soup, 80
    Quinoa with Spinach, 99
    Wild Salmon with Capers, 134–135

E
edamame
    Spicy Chicken Soup with Edamame, 67
eggplant
    Delectable Eggplant, 83–84
Eggplant Parmesan Lightened Up, 85
eggs
    Baked Eggs, 21
    Delicious Shirred Eggs, 23
    Easy Quiche, 26
    Garden Vegetable Crustless Quiche, 87
    Perfect Instant Pot Hard-Boiled Eggs, The, 19
    Poached Eggs, 20
    Spinach and Mushroom Frittata, 29
    To-Go Crustless Veggie Quiche Cups, 24–25
escarole
    Cannellini Bean Soup, 34

F
fish
    Caesar Salmon Fillets, 138
    Greek-Style Halibut Steaks, 130
    Herbed Fish Fillets, 129
    Lemon Pepper Tilapia, 123
    Maple-Glazed Salmon, 137
    Salmon with Chives, 133
    Simple Salmon, 131
    Wild Salmon with Capers, 134–135
fish sauce
    Napa Cabbage and Pork Soup, 79
Flavorful Tomato Soup, 49
Fresh Zucchini and Tomatoes, 140

G
Garden Vegetable Crustless Quiche, 87
Garden Vegetable Soup with Pasta, 54
Giant Healthy Pancake, 12
ginger
    Chicken Casablanca, 122
    Ginger Crumb Cake, 174
    Pumpkin Spice Pancake Bites, 13
    Spicy Chicken Soup with Edamame, 67
Ginger Crumb Cake, 174
Ginger Pork Chops, 111–112
Golden Millet, 168
Grain and Fruit Breakfast, 17
granola
    Breakfast Apples, 27
Greek-Style Halibut Steaks, 130
Green Bean and Ham Soup, 80

H
hake
    Herbed Fish Fillets, 129
halibut
    Greek-Style Halibut Steaks, 130
ham
    Easy Quiche, 26
    Napa Cabbage and Pork Soup, 80
    Senate Bean Soup, 77
Ham and Bean Soup, 75
Healthy Joes, 114
Hearty Vegetable Soup, 69
Herbed Fish Fillets, 129
Herbed Rice Pilaf, 155
Hometown Spanish Rice, 157
Hope's Family Hummus, 188
hummus

Hope's Family Hummus, 188

I

Indian Tomato Rice Soup, 42
Instant Pot Yogurt, 30
Instant Spaghetti Squash, 141
Insta-Oatmeal, 15
Insta Popcorn, 187
Italian Chicken and Broccoli, 125
Italian seasoning
    Italian Chicken and Broccoli, 125
    Stuffed Cabbage, 109–109
    Tomato Beef Soup, 74
    Turkey Peasant Soup, 60

J

jalapeño
    Chicken Chili Pepper Stew, 68
    Spicy Chicken Soup with Edamame, 67

K

kale
    Sweet Potato Soup with Kale, 46
ketchup
    Smoky Barbecue Meatballs, 191
    Turkey Meat Loaf, 126–127
    White Bean Soup, 33
Keto-Style Crème Brûlée, 178–179

L

leeks
    Cauliflower Mashed Potatoes, 147
Lemon Curry Rice Mix, 159
Lemon Pepper Tilapia, 123
Lentil, Spinach, and Rice Soup, 39
Lentil and Barley Soup, 38
Lentil Barley Stew with Chicken, 61
lentils
    Barbecue Lentils, 163
    Lentil and Barley Soup, 38
    Lentil Barley Stew with Chicken, 61
    Mediterranean Lentil Soup, 37
    Spiced Lentils with Chicken and Rice, 121
Lentils with Cheese, 102
Lighter Cream of Broccoli Soup, 51

M

mahi-mahi
    Herbed Fish Fillets, 129
Maple-Glazed Salmon, 137

maple syrup
    Cinnamon French Toast, 11
    Grain and Fruit Breakfast, 17
    Insta-Oatmeal, 15
    Maple-Glazed Salmon, 137
    Scrumptious Breakfast Barley, 16
marjoram
    Lentils with Cheese, 102
meatballs
    Smoky Barbecue Meatballs, 191
meat loaf
    Turkey Meat Loaf, 126–127
Mediterranean Lentil Soup, 37
Mexican-Inspired Bottom Round Roast, 106
millet
    Golden Millet, 168
    Grain and Fruit Breakfast, 17
Millet Casserole, 167
Moroccan Spiced Sweet Potato Medley, 86
muffins
    Apple Cranberry Muffin Bites, 197–198
Mushroom Risotto, 95
mushrooms
    Beef and Zucchini Casserole, 107
    Beef Mushroom Barley Soup, 72
    Chicken Dinner in a Packet, 115
    Chicken Rice Bake, 119
    Creamy Wild Rice Mushroom Soup, 43
    Easy Quiche, 26
    Garden Vegetable Crustless Quiche, 87
    Garden Vegetable Soup with Pasta, 54
    Pasta Primavera, 101
    Skinny Chicken Stroganoff, 117
    Spinach and Mushroom Frittata, 29
    Tomato and Barley Soup, 41
mustard
    Barbecue Lentils, 163
    Turkey Meat Loaf, 126–127

N

Napa Cabbage and Pork Soup, 79
noodles
    Chicken Noodle Soup, 63
    Garden Vegetable Soup with Pasta, 54
    Italian Chicken and Broccoli, 125
    Skinny Chicken Stroganoff, 117
    Veggie Minestrone, 57
nutmeg
    Ginger Crumb Cake, 174
    Orange-Glazed Parsnips, 152

Pumpkin Risotto, 96
Pumpkin Spice Pancake Bites, 13
Rice Pudding, 183
Turkey Meat Loaf, 126–127

O
oats
　Insta-Oatmeal, 15
Old Bay seasoning
　Simple Salmon, 131
Orange-Glazed Parsnips, 152
orange juice
　Apple Cranberry Muffin Bites, 197–198
　Orange-Glazed Parsnips, 152
oregano
　Barbacoa Beef, 103
　Beef and Zucchini Casserole, 107
　Black Bean Soup with Fresh Salsa, 35
　Chicken Noodle Soup, 63
　Flavorful Tomato Soup, 49
　Herbed Rice Pilaf, 155
　Lentil and Barley Soup, 38
　Sausage, Beans, and Rice Soup, 59
　Spinach Pie, 89
　Summer Squash Pie, 92
　Turkey Sausage and Cabbage Soup, 62

P
paprika
　Healthy Joes, 114
　Maple-Glazed Salmon, 137
　Sweet Potato Soup with Kale, 46
Paprika Pork Chops with Rice, 113
parsnips
　Orange-Glazed Parsnips, 152
　Vegetable Medley, 153
Pasta Primavera, 101
peas
　Mushroom Risotto, 95
　split
　　Lentil Barley Stew with Chicken, 61
pecans
　Scrumptious Breakfast Barley, 16
Perfect Instant Pot Hard-Boiled Eggs, 19
Perfect Sweet Potatoes, 145
pie
　Spinach Pie, 89
　Summer Squash Pie, 92
Poached Eggs, 20
popcorn

Insta Popcorn, 187
pork
　chops
　　Ginger Pork Chops, 111–112
　　Paprika Pork Chops with Rice, 113
　ground
　　Napa Cabbage and Pork Soup, 79
Potato and Spinach Soup, 45
potatoes
　Potato and Spinach Soup, 45
　sweet
　　Perfect Sweet Potatoes, 145
　　Sweet Potato Soup with Kale, 46
　　Sweet Potato Soup with Roasted Red Peppers
　　　& Vegetables, 47
　　White Bean Soup, 33
　Tomato Beef Soup, 74
pudding
　Coconut Rice Pudding, 181
　Rice Pudding, 183
　Tapioca Pudding, 184
pumpkin
　Zesty Pumpkin Soup, 55
Pumpkin Risotto, 96
Pumpkin Spice Pancake Bites, 13

Q
quinoa
　Grain and Fruit Breakfast, 17
Quinoa with Spinach, 99

R
raisins
　Chicken Casablanca, 122
　golden
　　Curried Barley, 165
　　Lemon Curry Rice Mix, 159
　Moroccan Spiced Sweet Potato Medley, 86
　Rice Pudding, 183
　Spiced Lentils with Chicken and Rice, 121
　Squash Apple Bake, 143
rice
　arborio
　　Coconut Rice Pudding, 181
　　Mushroom Risotto, 95
　　Pumpkin Risotto, 96
　basmati
　　Indian Tomato Rice Soup, 42
　brown
　　Apple-Cranberry Wild Rice, 161

Artichokes and Brown Rice, 160
Beef and Zucchini Casserole, 107
Cheesy Chicken and Rice, 120
Grain and Fruit Breakfast, 17
Herbed Rice Pilaf, 155
Lemon Curry Rice Mix, 159
Lentil, Spinach, and Rice Soup, 39
Paprika Pork Chops with Rice, 113
Rice Pudding, 183
Sausage, Beans, and Rice Soup, 59
Spiced Lentils with Chicken and Rice, 121
Stuffed Cabbage, 109–109
Stuffed Sweet Pepper Soup, 71
Hometown Spanish Rice, 157
jasmine
Cilantro Lime Rice, 156
wild
Apple-Cranberry Wild Rice, 161
Rice Pudding, 183
risotto
Barley Risotto with Grilled Peppers, 97
Mushroom Risotto, 95
Pumpkin Risotto, 96
rosemary
Lentil and Barley Soup, 38
Sweet Potato Soup with Kale, 46
Rosemary Carrots, 151

sage
Lentils with Cheese, 102
Senate Bean Soup, 77
salmon
Caesar Salmon Fillets, 138
Maple-Glazed Salmon, 137
Simple Salmon, 131
Wild Salmon with Capers, 134–135
Salmon with Chives, 133
salsa
Beef and Black Bean Chili, 73
Mexican-Inspired Bottom Round Roast, 106
Millet Casserole, 167
sausage
Easy Quiche, 26
turkey
Sausage, Beans, and Rice Soup, 59
Turkey Peasant Soup, 60
Turkey Sausage and Cabbage Soup, 62
Sausage, Beans, and Rice Soup, 59
savory

Apple-Cranberry Wild Rice, 161
scallions
Ginger Pork Chops, 111–112
Quinoa with Spinach, 99
Scrumptious Breakfast Barley, 16
Seasoned Beets, 144
Senate Bean Soup, 77
sherry
Mediterranean Lentil Soup, 37
Simple Salmon, 131
Skinny Chicken Stroganoff, 117
Smoky Barbecue Meatballs, 191
soup
Beef Mushroom Barley Soup, 72
Black Bean Soup with Fresh Salsa, 35
Cannellini Bean Soup, 34
Chicken Barley Soup, 65
Chicken Chili Pepper Stew, 68
Chicken Noodle Soup, 63
Creamy Asparagus Soup, 50
Creamy Wild Rice Mushroom Soup, 43
Curried Carrot Bisque, 53
Flavorful Tomato Soup, 49
Garden Vegetable Soup with Pasta, 54
Ham and Bean Soup, 75
Hearty Vegetable Soup, 69
Indian Tomato Rice Soup, 42
Lentil, Spinach, and Rice Soup, 39
Lentil and Barley Soup, 38
Lentil Barley Stew with Chicken, 61
Lighter Cream of Broccoli Soup, 51
Mediterranean Lentil Soup, 37
Napa Cabbage and Pork Soup, 79
Potato and Spinach Soup, 45
Sausage, Beans, and Rice Soup, 59
Senate Bean Soup, 77
Spicy Chicken Soup with Edamame, 67
Stuffed Sweet Pepper Soup, 71
Sweet Potato Soup with Kale, 46
Sweet Potato Soup with Roasted Red Peppers &
Vegetables, 47
Tomato and Barley Soup, 41
Tomato Beef Soup, 74
Turkey Peasant Soup, 60
Turkey Sausage and Cabbage Soup, 62
Veggie Minestrone, 57
White Bean Soup, 33
Zesty Pumpkin Soup, 55
sour cream
Black Bean Soup with Fresh Salsa, 35

Skinny Chicken Stroganoff, 117
Spinach and Artichoke Dip, 189
Summer Squash Pie, 92
Sour Cream Corn Bread, 194–195
soy sauce
Caesar Salmon Fillets, 138
Ginger Pork Chops, 111–112
Herbed Rice Pilaf, 155
Spiced Lentils with Chicken and Rice, 121
Spicy Chicken Soup with Edamame, 67
spinach
Lentil, Spinach, and Rice Soup, 39
Potato and Spinach Soup, 45
Quinoa with Spinach, 99
Spinach and Mushroom Frittata, 29
To-Go Crustless Veggie Quiche Cups, 24–25
Turkey Peasant Soup, 60
Veggie Minestrone, 57
Spinach and Artichoke Dip, 189
Spinach and Mushroom Frittata, 29
Spinach Pie, 89
Spinach Stuffed Tomatoes, 90–91
squash
Instant Spaghetti Squash, 141
Summer Squash Pie, 92
Squash Apple Bake, 143
strawberry jam
Dessert Filled Apples, 177
Strawberry Shortcake, 175
Stuffed Cabbage, 109–109
Stuffed Sweet Pepper Soup, 71
Summer Squash Pie, 92
sweet potato
Perfect Sweet Potatoes, 145
Sweet Potato Soup with Kale, 46
Sweet Potato Soup with Roasted Red Peppers &
Vegetables, 47
White Bean Soup, 33
Sweet Potato Soup with Kale, 46
Sweet Potato Soup with Roasted Red Peppers &
Vegetables, 47

T
tamari
Caesar Salmon Fillets, 138
Ginger Pork Chops, 111–112
Tapioca Pudding, 184
tarragon
Salmon with Chives, 133
Tasty Tofu Brownie Snacks, 170–171

thyme
Creamy Wild Rice Mushroom Soup, 43
Flavorful Tomato Soup, 49
Herbed Rice Pilaf, 155
Lentils with Cheese, 102
Mediterranean Lentil Soup, 37
White Bean Soup, 33
tilapia
Lemon Pepper Tilapia, 123
tofu
Tasty Tofu Brownie Snacks, 170–171
To-Go Crustless Veggie Quiche Cups, 24–25
Tomato and Barley Soup, 41
Tomato Beef Soup, 74
tomatoes
Chicken Barley Soup, 65
Flavorful Tomato Soup, 49
Fresh Zucchini and Tomatoes, 140
Garden Vegetable Soup with Pasta, 54
Greek-Style Halibut Steaks, 130
Healthy Joes, 114
Hearty Vegetable Soup, 69
Hometown Spanish Rice, 157
Indian Tomato Rice Soup, 42
Lentil, Spinach, and Rice Soup, 39
Lentil and Barley Soup, 38
Lentils with Cheese, 102
Mediterranean Lentil Soup, 37
Millet Casserole, 167
Moroccan Spiced Sweet Potato Medley, 86
Paprika Pork Chops with Rice, 113
Sausage, Beans, and Rice Soup, 59
Spinach Stuffed Tomatoes, 90–91
Sweet Potato Soup with Kale, 46
Sweet Potato Soup with Roasted Red Peppers &
Vegetables, 47
Tomato and Barley Soup, 41
Tomato Beef Soup, 74
Turkey Peasant Soup, 60
Turkey Sausage and Cabbage Soup, 62
Veggie Minestrone, 57
Wild Salmon with Capers, 134–135
tomato sauce
Barbecue Lentils, 163
Delectable Eggplant, 83–84
Eggplant Parmesan Lightened Up, 85
Healthy Joes, 114
turkey
ground
Hearty Vegetable Soup, 69

Turkey Meat Loaf, 126–127
Turkey Peasant Soup, 60
Turkey Sausage and Cabbage Soup, 62
turnip
    Vegetable Medley, 153

V
Vegetable Medley, 153
Veggie Minestrone, 57

W
walnuts
    Tasty Tofu Brownie Snacks, 170–171
White Bean Soup, 33
Wild Salmon with Capers, 134–135
wine
    white
        Pumpkin Risotto, 96
        Wild Salmon with Capers, 134–135

Y
yogurt
    Apple Cranberry Muffin Bites, 197–198
    Instant Pot Yogurt, 30

Z
Zesty Pumpkin Soup, 55
zucchini
    Beef and Zucchini Casserole, 107
    Chicken Casablanca, 122
    Chicken Dinner in a Packet, 115
    Fresh Zucchini and Tomatoes, 140
    Garden Vegetable Crustless Quiche, 87
    Greek-Style Halibut Steaks, 130
    Healthy Joes, 114
    Pasta Primavera, 101
    Turkey Peasant Soup, 60

About the Author

Hope Comerford is a mom, wife, elementary music teacher, blogger, recipe developer, public speaker, Young Living Essential Oils essential oil enthusiast/educator, and published author. In 2013, she was diagnosed with a severe gluten intolerance and since then has spent many hours creating easy, practical, and delicious gluten-free recipes that can be enjoyed by both those who are affected by gluten and those who are not.

Growing up, Hope spent many hours in the kitchen with her Meme (grandmother), and her love for cooking grew from there. While working on her master's degree when her daughter was young, Hope turned to her slow cookers for some salvation and sanity. It was from there she began truly experimenting with recipes and quickly learned she had the ability to get a little more creative in the kitchen and develop her own recipes.

In 2010, Hope started her blog, *A Busy Mom's Slow Cooker Adventures*, to simply share the recipes she was making with her family and friends. She never imagined people all over the world would begin visiting her page and sharing her recipes with others as well. In 2013, Hope self-published her first cookbook, *Slow Cooker Recipes 10 Ingredients or Less and Gluten-Free*, and then later wrote *The Gluten-Free Slow Cooker*.

Hope became the new brand ambassador and author of Fix-It and Forget-It in mid-2016. Since then, she has brought her excitement and creativeness to the Fix-It and Forget-It brand. Through Fix-It and Forget-It, she has written *Fix-It and Forget-It Healthy Slow Cooker Cookbook*, *Fix-It and Forget-It Healthy 5-Ingredient Cookbook*, *Fix-It and Forget-It Instant Pot Cookbook*, *Fix-It and Forget-It Plant-Based Comfort Foods Cookbook*, *Fix-it and Forget-It Keto Plant-Based Cookbook*, *Fix-It and Forget-It Instant Pot Diabetes Cookbook*, and many more.

Hope lives in the city of Clinton Township, Michigan, near Metro Detroit. She has been happily married to her husband and best friend, Justin, since 2008. Together they have two children, Ella and Gavin, who are her motivation, inspiration, and heart. In her spare time, Hope enjoys traveling, singing, cooking, spending time with friends and family, working out, and relaxing.